UP

YOUR

OPTIMISM

GAME

UP YOUR OPTIMISM GAME

How to Turn Stress, Depression, and Anxiety into **Joy, Happiness, and Peace of Mind**

CHARLES INNISS

WREN HOUSE
press

UP YOUR OPTIMISM GAME
How to Turn Stress, Depression, and Anxiety
into Joy, Happiness, and Peace of Mind
First Edition

ISBN   978-1-967115-29-7 *Hardcover*
       978-1-967115-28-0 *Paperback*
       978-1-967115-27-3 *Ebook*

LCCN 2026903336

*For all those who dare to shine a little
brighter and light the way for others*

CONTENTS

Part IV. The Magic: Putting It All Together   273

INTRODUCTION

It happens so fast.

One day, you're a kid without a care in the world. You're so full of energy and joy that you laugh and smile effortlessly. You're daring, creative, and curious about life. Hope drives you to chase crazy dreams, and—with fearless determination—you ascend the academic ranks and earn multiple degrees on your way to becoming a successful adult.

And then you wake up one day and think to yourself, *Damn, adulting kinda sucks!*

Anxiety and worry become your two best friends. Stress feels like a crazy ex you keep trying to break up with, to no avail. Life throws so much loss and heartbreak your way that sometimes you just want to curl up in a ball and stay in bed all day.

One day, you're happy playing with sticks and rocks; the next, you're miserable and depressed.

One day, you're so confident and bold that you'll wear butterfly wings to kindergarten; the next, you feel like an impostor in your own skin.

One day, you're hopeful and full of life; the next, you feel completely drained and hopeless.

Is it just me, or did anyone else miss the college class where they teach you what to do when breakups, health problems, and financial setbacks turn your life upside down?

College doesn't teach us how to be happy. It teaches us how to be good at our jobs. So, we become good teachers, engineers, lawyers, doctors, and corporate professionals, but we still struggle with burnout, depression, and anxiety. And we're left to learn about mental health and emotional well-being at the School of Hard Knocks.

Adulthood doesn't have to be this way. You can have so much joy running through your veins that the littlest things make you smile. You can have so much confidence in yourself that nothing holds you back from your dreams. You can have so much poise that you stay grounded and strong through any adversity.

All you have to do is up your optimism game.

Mental health revolves around two buckets: (1) cognitive function and (2) positive emotion. Cognitive function involves your ability to focus, remember things, and perform activities that require mental skill. Positive emotion refers to how good you feel emotionally. Sometimes, our brains function well, but we use them in ways that lead us to feel more negative emotions like worry, anger, or hopelessness.

Optimism is generally defined as hopefulness and confidence about the future, but I use a broader definition. My definition of optimism is any thinking pattern (or action) that helps create positive emotions—and teaching you how to increase *your* positive emotions is the goal of this book!

Your family needs you at your best, the world needs you at your best, and *you* need you at your best. So, I'm going to show you how you can use the power of optimism to transform your stress, depression, and anxiety into joy, happiness, and peace of mind—allowing you to make the biggest possible positive impact at home, at work, and in the world, without compromising your own mental health.

In addition to teaching you about your twenty-four Optimism Muscles (bet you didn't even know you had these!), I'm going to do the following:

- Explain the anatomy of your inner world, so you can navigate your emotions with ease
- Show you how to train your brain to automatically generate a wide variety of positive emotions using my Think, Speak, Write Mindset Workout Method
- Give you a six-week Optimism Challenge to help you reclaim your joy and peace

Optimism can transform your life in many ways. It can boost your confidence and motivation, strengthen your relationship with yourself and others, and be a leadership superpower. The practices I'll share have worked for my clients, and I know they can also work for you.

Optimism Workouts

Everybody knows if you want good physical health, you have to work out your body. The premise of this book is simple: If you want good mental health, you have to work out your mind.

The question is: *How?*

In a way, I've been working to answer this question my whole life. My passion for health and wellness began at an early age. Growing up as an athlete in New Orleans, I was often injured. When a physical therapist helped me return to basketball, I decided that I also wanted to contribute to the world by helping people to get rid of pain. So, I headed north to earn my doctorate in physical therapy at Boston University, and Boston has been my home ever since.

When I began my career as a physical therapist and personal trainer, I was obsessed with anatomy and physiology. And when Blue Cross Blue Shield of Massachusetts hired me as the on-site corporate wellness coach for employees, I leaned on my knowledge of the body to help my clients to get healthier. But as more professionals came to me with stress-related concerns, I realized emotional wellness was just as important as physical wellness, which inspired my passion for positive psychology.

Diving into positive psychology research, I was fascinated with the power of optimism to motivate people to pursue behavior change. As I read more about the benefits of optimism for physical and mental health, I became convinced that optimism was the most powerful wellness tool anyone could possess.

One problem: How could I help people get it and grow it?

Many fitness books teach physical anatomy and include workout plans to help people transform their bodies. But I couldn't find the equivalent when it came to mental health. So, I used my love of anatomy and coaching experience to create a fitness-like approach to mental health that would be simple to understand and easy to practice.

Optimism workouts were the solution my clients needed—and also the one I needed.

When I found out my position was being eliminated during the height of the COVID-19 pandemic, a wave of depression hit me. For months, my routine turned into this unhealthy loop: Get up, eat chocolate, binge Netflix, take a nap, eat more chocolate, binge more Netflix. I watched so much Netflix that I had to start finding series in other languages, because I'd finished all the good ones in English!

Then one day, I was scrolling through YouTube and came across a video featuring a yogi who said, "Joy or misery is your choice." I had heard this type of message before, but this time it just hit me: I didn't have to wallow on the couch and eat chocolate all day. I had agency over how I lived my life.

So, I started coaching myself. First, I began exercising my body, and my energy started coming back. But I knew I also needed to exercise my mind. That's when I created my first personal Mindset Workout routine. I started a gratitude journal, did breathing exercises, and listened to and repeated positive affirmations—and I noticed my mindset shifting.

My joy, hope, and optimism started coming back, thanks to my optimism workouts. During a hard time when my life was far from perfect, I had so much joy and energy that I popped out of bed at 5:00 a.m., smiled randomly, and found a new purpose that fired me up: spreading hope and optimism as far and wide as I could.

Because I know what it's like to struggle with mental health challenges, I felt called to write this book to help people like you. I spent the first half of my career creating workouts to help people transform their bodies. Now, as an optimism and mental health coach, I've created a six-week optimism workout program to help you transform your mind.

At its core, this is a coaching book, so think of me as your coach. Since coaching is collaborative, I want to encourage you to apply your own wisdom to what you read. Coaching is also forward-looking and action-oriented—so focus on the changes you'd like to make, and put what you learn into practice. What coaching is *not*, however, is a substitute for therapy or medical advice. If you are dealing with a serious mental illness, please seek counsel from a licensed practitioner.

Throughout the book, you'll meet different "clients," but you'll mostly follow the journey of two main characters, Kristen and Joe, who represent the most typical clients I've worked with. I hope you gain insights from their experiences and feel inspired by their transformations.

Adulting doesn't have to suck. You can live a full life, feel great emotionally, and be a bright light for others. I know you have your own unique challenges, but I also know that you've already accomplished many things in your life. So, I'm confident that you can learn how to use the power of optimism to decrease your stress, depression, and anxiety.

More joy, happiness, and peace could be just a few mental workouts away, so let's dive in!

THE MIND
MASTERING YOUR INNER WORLD

My favorite college class was gross anatomy (anatomical structures visible to the naked eye), and to help pay for grad school, I dissected cadavers and taught gross anatomy labs. I love anatomy. When you can see how muscles are connected to joints, you can make exercise recommendations to improve performance or decrease pain.

When I worked in a spine clinic, patients would often come in with pain between their shoulder blades, and I would tell them it was related to their neck. Sometimes, they'd look at me funny and say, "But Doc, my neck doesn't hurt." Then I'd show them that the muscles supporting their head and neck were anchored between their shoulder blades, and they'd understand the connection.

Knowing how your body is organized can help you maintain physical health. By the same token, knowing how your mind is organized can help you maintain mental health. Once you understand the anatomy of your inner world, you can navigate your emotions with more skill and ease.

In addition to teaching you the anatomy of your emotions, thoughts, motivation, and stress, Part 1 will show you the role optimism plays in decreasing emotional pain and increasing your joy, happiness, and peace.

ONE

THE ANATOMY OF EMOTION

*"I am not afraid of storms, for I am
learning how to sail my ship."*
—LOUISA MAY ALCOTT

WHEN I FIRST MET KRISTEN, SHE HAD JUST CELE-brated her fortieth birthday. And if you looked at her social media posts, you would think her life was perfect. She had the house, the degrees, the family, and the career. But even though she was a highly educated and successful professional, she still struggled emotionally.

Between working full-time, caring for her daughters, trying to stay healthy, and just wanting to be a good wife, daughter, and friend, Kristen's life was a whirlwind. She often felt stressed and overwhelmed, and her anxiety started affecting her marriage and work performance.

Like many clients, Kristen was her own worst critic, and internally, she was really negative toward herself. She felt her body was flawed, she felt she wasn't smart enough at work, and she always felt she wasn't doing enough for her kids, spouse, or parents. Some days, she secretly wished that she didn't have kids, and others, she wished she'd win the lottery so she could just relax on the beach and drink mai tais.

But Kristen wasn't always this way. When she was younger, she was full of joy and big dreams. For an assignment in eighth grade, she wrote, "When I grow up, I want to be an Olympic soccer player, a singer, a doctor, and an amazing mom who teaches her children that anything is possible...and most of all, I want to be happy." Young Kristen was full of hope and optimism. But now at forty, she was disillusioned by what her life had become, a seemingly never-ending list of problems and obligations that often left her physically and mentally drained.

She had almost given up on feeling happy. But when she heard me speak about the power of optimism at a company wellness event, she started to feel hopeful that she could learn how to overcome her mental challenges and become the person she'd envisioned when she was younger and full of life.

Throughout this book, I'm going to share with you the same ideas, principles, and mental workouts that I taught Kristen to help her find her spark, step into her confidence, and reclaim her joy! She transformed by learning how to master her inner emotional game, and now it's time for you to master yours too.

The Mind-Body-Behavior Wheel

Have you ever asked yourself where emotions come from? It's not like you can buy them from a store, although it would be cool if Amazon could ship you a bottle of confidence, a box of joy, or a bag of inner peace. Instead of a warehouse, emotions come from inside of you—and when you master your inner world, it can feel like you're constantly being delivered packages of positive feelings.

Emotions arise from the interplay between your mind, body, and behavior—all of which you have some agency over. To illustrate the anatomy of emotion, I developed the Mind-Body-Behavior Wheel.

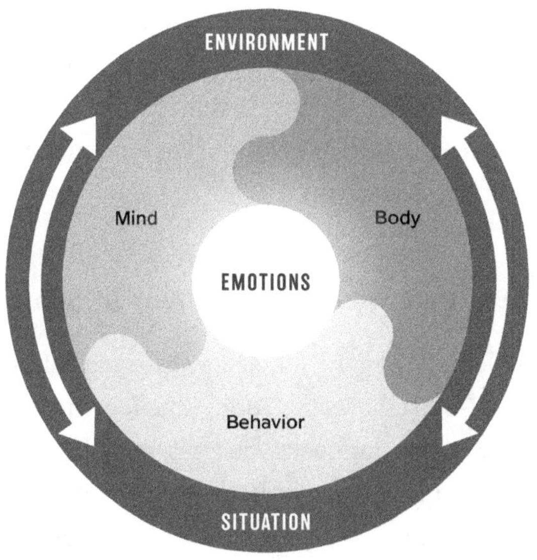

Your emotions are at the center of the wheel and have a bidirectional relationship with your mind, body, and behavior. Mind, body, and behavior also have bidirectional relationships with each other. Mind affects body and behavior. Body affects mind and behavior. And behavior affects body and mind. Everything is connected, and a negative or positive change in any area can start your emotional wheel rolling backward or forward.

Now, you may be thinking, *But Charles, what about the environment and external factors?* Two observations: First, the environment affects mind, body, and behavior. Second, from a coaching and empowerment perspective, it's better to focus on what you can control. Environment does play a role, but you also have power over your emotions—and I want you to lean into your power.

You can influence your emotional state through how you take care of your body, what you do, and how you think. I refer to these strategies as Body Care, Behavior Care (aka Soul Care), and Mind Care, and they're all part of your emotional self-care tool kit. Let's break each one down.

Body Care: Your Body and Your Emotions

Have you ever felt "hangry" (angry because you're hungry)? My friend has a T-shirt that says, "Forgive me for what I said when I was hangry." If someone asks you a silly question when you're well fed and rested, you're likely to be patient and understanding, indulging multiple follow-ups. But change what's happening in your body so that you're tired and depleted, and an innocent question can trigger outrage.

The brain evolved to regulate your body, and your mood is directly tied to what's happening in your body. Sometimes, your body is the key driver of your emotional experience. When your body experiences a negative physical state like hunger, fatigue, pain, or disease (a state of dis-ease), you'll feel more negative emotions. And when your body is in a pleasant or healthy state, you'll feel more positive emotions.

You can see this in the hangry example: What's happening in your body (your physiological state) precedes your mood (emotions), thinking, and behavior. So, shifting the physical state of your body through Body Care can influence how you feel, think, and behave.

In Chapter 31, we'll discuss how the five pillars of Body Care (nutrition, movement, breathing, nature, and sleep) help create feelings of joy and peace. But for now, just note that your body is a major source of your emotions, and anything you do to care for your body will affect your mind.

The reverse is also true. Your thoughts affect what happens in your body. In a study conducted at Columbia University,* people were given a milkshake labeled "Indulgence: Decadence You Deserve." According to the nutrition label shown to the participants, the shake had 620 calories and 30 grams of fat.

Researchers found that the hunger hormone, ghrelin, dropped significantly after participants drank the 620-calorie shake. A week later, the same participants were given a milkshake labeled "Sensi-Shake: Guilt Free Satisfaction," which claimed to have only 140 calories and 0 grams of fat. When participants drank the low-calorie shake, there wasn't a significant change in ghrelin levels.

---

*   Alia J. Crum et al., "Mind over Milkshakes: Mindsets, Not Just Nutrients, Determine Ghrelin Response," *Health Psychology* 30, no. 4 (July 2011): 424–31, https://doi.org/10.1037/a0023467.

These responses make sense based on physiological knowledge: Lots of calories result in lower levels of hunger hormones, while just a few calories create barely any change in hunger hormone levels.

But there's a twist: The nutrition labels were made up to affect the thinking of the participants. Both times, they actually drank the same 380-calorie milkshake.

Wait, what?

That's right: Different thoughts led to different physiological responses. When people thought they were drinking lots of calories, their digestive hormones responded one way. But when they thought they were drinking just a few calories, their digestive systems responded another way, despite the fact that the inputs were identical.

How can this be? Many top neuroscientists believe the brain's default mode is prediction and correction, not stimulus and response. In other words, instead of reacting to inputs after they happen, it's more efficient for the brain to regulate your body by anticipating where to send resources ahead of time based on all the information it has, past and present.

Have you ever typed one letter into the Google search bar and magically the exact thing you were thinking popped up as an autosuggestion? Freaky, right?! Well, your brain is the OG of supercomputers, and it's always running predictive algorithms.

In her book *How Emotions Are Made*, Dr. Lisa Feldman Barrett presents her theory of constructed emotion, which says, in part, that our emotions are created by our past experiences and concepts.

To regulate your body and emotions, your brain uses concepts as shortcuts, which is exactly what computers do. Based on your demographic data (e.g., age, sex, location) and behavioral data (e.g., search history, purchases, time on sites), the computer first develops a concept of who you are, and then it tries to anticipate what you need and present it via autosuggestion.

Similarly, your brain uses your past experiences, sensory inputs, and especially current thoughts to influence your physical responses. Just like your thoughts can affect how your digestive hormones respond, thoughts can also affect how your stress hormones, immune system, nervous system, and cardiovascular system respond. Your thoughts can help you heal, and your thoughts can make you sick. Your thoughts can give you energy, and your thoughts can drain the life out of you.

There is an intimate connection between body and mind that cannot be separated. Some of your joy is created by your body, so to feel your best emotionally, you'll need a little Body Care. Kristen was familiar with this type of self-care, and to get her emotional wheel rolling in a positive direction, I encouraged her to keep taking care of her body. Then, to really get her joy flowing, I invited her to start engaging in more behaviors that fed her soul.

Behavior Care, aka Soul Care:
Your Behavior and Your Emotions

This is going to sound so simple that I almost don't want to say it, but here goes: When you do things that make you happy, you'll likely feel happy—and when you don't do things that make you happy, you'll probably feel less happy.

I love bowling and was the captain of my high school bowling team. When I was in college, I regularly went bowling with my friends at Lanes and Games in Alewife, a neighborhood of Cambridge, Massachusetts. That was our spot. But once I graduated and started working, I didn't make time for this fun hobby. When my aunt heard me talking about being stressed at work, she'd remind me how much I loved bowling and nudge me to go play.

We adults often become less joyful because we stop doing things that make us joyful. Working and caregiving can pull us away from activities that naturally lead to positive emotions. For instance, music was a big part of Kristen's life when she was younger. She wrote her own songs and played guitar, but once she got married and had kids, that part of her soul ended up in the closet next to her guitar.

Just as you need to feed and take care of your body, you also need to feed your soul. If you want to feel more inspired and energized, you have to do what makes you come alive. And to feel more joyful, you must spend some time doing what makes your heart sing.

If you're feeling depressed, unsatisfied, or uninspired, those could be signals that you need to spend more time on soul-caring behaviors. Reengaging with an old hobby or passion, serving something greater than yourself, and connecting with others are all great ways to feed your soul. I'll talk more about the three pillars of Soul Care in Chapter 32—flow, connection, and contribution—but for now, remember that

Behavior Care and Soul Care address the same part of the Mind-Body-Behavior Wheel. You'll see me use both terms over the course of the book, depending on what we're working out.

Mind Care: Your Thoughts and Emotions

While body and behavior play a crucial role in the creation of your emotions, your mind plays the most important role. Like many of us, Kristen neglected Mind Care, and this self-care mistake was taking a toll.

Whenever she felt stressed, her friends would tell her to meditate or get a massage, and her doctor would tell her to exercise and get better sleep. Those suggestions are all wonderful Body Care strategies that can positively influence emotions, especially if the stress mostly stems from your body. However, you can work out and get a massage but still feel anxiety when asked to give a presentation if the stress originates in your mind.

This was the case for Kristen. Many of her negative emotions stemmed from her thinking. To help her make her biggest emotional breakthroughs, we decided to focus more on Mind Care.

Because of my background as a physical therapist, here's the analogy I used to help Kristen think about her mental health: Just as you have physical muscles, you also have mental muscles. Your physical muscles generate movement, and your mental muscles generate emotions.

Your mental muscles can be divided into two categories:

- **Optimism Muscles** generate positive emotions, like joy, happiness, and peace.
- **Pessimism Muscles** generate negative emotions, like depression, anxiety, and anger.

You need both sets of muscles to move through life. The strength of pessimism and negativity is that they serve to protect you and keep you safe. Anger helps you fight, and fear helps you flee. But while your negativity bias exists to help you survive, you need optimism to thrive. If you want to feel more positive emotions, you have to strengthen the mental muscles—or thinking patterns—that generate those positive emotions.

Your twenty-four Optimism Muscles are gratitude, self-appreciation, appreciation of others, vision, mindfulness, savoring, celebration (and appreciation), joy, humor (and fun), love, self-compassion, confidence, courage, awe (and wonder), serenity (and acceptance), agency (and empowerment), empathy, agreeableness, forgiveness, meaning-making (and purpose), dreaming (and imagination), passion (and interest), faith (and trust), and hope. In Part 3, I've devoted a full chapter to each one, so you'll feel confident in building them, just like Kristen learned to do.

To transform her stress, depression, and anxiety, we focused a little on Body Care and Soul Care—and a lot more on Mind Care. We'll dive deeper into exactly how we did this in the coming chapters, but to finish off this chapter, let's look at how you can use the Mind-Body-Behavior Wheel to turn negative emotions like stress, depression, and anxiety into joy, happiness, and peace.

Transforming Negative Emotions

Emotions can be complex, but keeping it simple, they are signals about your needs. When your needs are being met, you feel positive emotions. When your needs are not being met, you feel negative ones. You have physical needs (e.g., nutrition, sleep, comfort), social needs (e.g., connection, belonging), and psychological needs (e.g., growth, safety). The more mindful you are about your needs, the easier it is to make choices that positively affect your emotions.

We'll expand on these concepts throughout the book, but for now here are some simple ways you can use your mind, body, or behavior to transform common negative emotions like depression, anxiety, and burnout.

Transforming Depression into Joy

Mind

Pessimism makes you depressed, and constantly focusing on negatives can spoil your mood. To shift depression through your mind, practice focusing on positives like what you're grateful for. Many studies show that practicing gratitude can be an effective strategy to combat depression.

Body

Depression is a low-energy, negative emotion. In addition to increasing "feel good" hormones, regular exercise increases your body's ability to produce energy. Sometimes, feeling depressed is a signal that you need more movement and energy in your body.

Behavior

To shift depression through your actions, feed your soul. You can engage in hobbies and pursue passions. You can actively cultivate connections with others and ask for support. Or you can find a way to contribute and serve something greater than yourself.

You don't have to do everything. Sometimes, one positive change like gratitude, exercise, or connection can get you rolling in a positive direction!

Transforming Anxiety into Calm

Mind

Pessimism makes you anxious because that's its job. Worry and fear help you survive. I'll expand on this when we explore the anatomy of stress (Chapter 4), but here's the big idea: Instead of always focusing on the worst-case scenario, you can *decatastrophize* by thinking about best-case and likely scenarios.

Body

While depression is a low-energy negative emotion, anxiety is a high-energy negative emotion. Slow, deep breathing can calm anxiety by decreasing the energy in your body. A massage or soak in a hot bath with Epsom salts and lavender can also help you relax.

Behavior

Another way to calm anxiety is through your actions. Try decreasing stimulation from technology and scheduling more quiet time. If your anxiety comes from not being good at something, you can increase that skill and ability. Or you can connect with and lean on others for support.

Transforming Burnout into Energy

Mind

Your mindset toward success influences burnout. If you think you have to know everything, do everything, and fix everything, that mindset will never let you rest. Letting go of a need to do everything and adopting stories like "I am enough" can decrease burnout and overwhelm.

Body

Too much exercise (overtraining) or too little exercise can lead to burnout, so get the right dose. You can practice sensory deprivation in a float tank to let your central nervous system rest. Eating a nutritious diet, getting adequate sleep, and many other Body Care activities can also help with burnout.

Behavior

If you're overloaded, it's a signal that there is too much for the body and mind to handle as well as too many behaviors to do. You only have so much time, physical energy, and mental bandwidth, but you can get better at simplifying, setting boundaries, saying no, letting go, offloading activities, and not putting yourself last.

I Nominate You as Captain

Those are just some ideas for how you can exercise power over your emotions. I'm sure you're already doing some of them, and I know you have additional wisdom you can apply to the Mind-Body-Behavior Wheel concept.

Now, you're equipped with a basic map to sail the seas of your emotional world. Winds in your environment may blow you off course and nudge you toward stress, depression, and anxiety, but as the captain of your emotional ship, you can deploy Body Care, Behavior/Soul Care, and Mind Care to navigate yourself to joy, happiness, and peace.

If you're just learning to sail, that's okay—stick with me over these next chapters as we dive deeper into your inner world to explore your thoughts, motivation, and stress.

 **UP YOUR OPTIMISM GAME: COACH'S CORNER** 

Think of one activity in each category—Body Care, Behavior Care, and Mind Care—that will positively influence your emotions. Make them a part of your emotional self-care tool kit. Depending on the situation, you can choose the strategy that best fits your needs. You don't have to be afraid of life's storms, because you can learn how to sail your own ship.

TWO

THE ANATOMY OF THINKING

"Our life is what our thoughts make it."
—MARCUS AURELIUS

"I COULD HAVE DONE MORE TO PREVENT MY DIVORCE," Joe said.

"Oh?" I asked. "How so?"

"I was too cynical, and too angry all the time," he admitted. After a long pause, he added, "I still am."

At age fifty-two, Joe was referred to me by his lifestyle medicine physician, Dr. Dave, because of physical problems related to stress. He'd gained weight and had trouble sleeping, and his blood pressure kept creeping up. Dr. Dave thought a coach could help Joe find his motivation and better manage his emotions, especially anger.

Initially, Joe was skeptical that talking with someone about his emotions could help him sleep better, but he respected his doctor and didn't want to rely on blood pressure medication. He was also finally dating someone seriously and didn't want to repeat the same patterns that contributed to the failure of his first marriage. He wanted to learn how to combat his anger and stress so that he could feel better physically, have stronger relationships, and become a more effective leader. So, he decided to give coaching a try.

Joe grew up in Atlanta with his single mom and was bullied in school. When he hit a growth spurt, he turned to football and vowed that no one would ever bully him again. He learned at a young age that people had to be tough to be taken seriously. Because his mom struggled financially, he wanted a career that made a lot of money, so he pursued MBA and law degrees to put himself on a high-earning path. Law school led him to Boston, where he eventually became VP of sales at a technology company.

As a former athlete, Joe was extremely competitive. He brought his drive to be the best into his role as a leader and pushed his team hard. He hated when people made mistakes, distrusted others, and was cynical about the world. The positive spin on those attributes could be high standards, quality execution, and discernment, but taken to an extreme, they were sapping the joy and ease from Joe's life. He needed help to shift his approach.

Whether you're more outwardly negative toward the world like Joe or more inwardly negative toward yourself like Kristen, the key to your success, thriving, and happiness—I humbly proclaim—is figuring out how to up your optimism game!

If I had to choose one word to describe the anatomy of thinking, it would be *mindset*. Your mindset is a product of your focus and your story. What you focus on affects how you feel, and the story you tell yourself about what you focus on also affects how you feel. Thinking affects everything, and from a cognitive perspective, your emotions are created by your focus and story. To test this out, let's do a quick mental experiment.

The Power of Focus to Influence Emotions

Think about someone you're close to. Then, think about a time when they hurt you, disappointed you, or let you down. What emotions come up when you focus on a negative interaction with this person—anger, sadness, disgust, frustration, or something else?

Now, while keeping the same person in mind, think about a time when they had your back, were totally there for you, and were your rock! What emotions come up when you focus on a positive interaction with this person—maybe gratitude, love, joy, or connection?

If you played along with this exercise, you may have gone from anger and sadness to love and joy in a matter of seconds, just as a result of shifting your focus.

A positive focus leads to positive emotions, whereas a negative focus leads to negative emotions. Training your brain to spend more time focusing on positives doesn't mean negatives don't exist. Every person has positives and negatives. Every situation has pluses and minuses. Every choice has pros and cons. And your emotions are influenced by which aspect you focus on.

We all develop physical and mental habits. If you've gotten into the habit of focusing more on negatives, you can exercise your positive focus to generate more joy and peace.

The Power of Story to Influence Emotions

In a noteworthy study on the relationship between thinking and satisfaction, researchers combed through hundreds of pictures of Olympic medal winners standing on the podium in an attempt to determine their happiness levels based on the quality of their smiles. Unsurprisingly, the researchers found that, on average, gold medalists had the biggest, brightest smiles. But surprisingly, on average, bronze medalists had bigger smiles than silver medalists.*

In addition to focus, the story you tell yourself shapes your emotions. The gold medalists' story probably sounded something like this: *Yes, I did it! All my hard work and dedication paid off and helped me win gold.* The bronze medalists' story maybe sounded something like this: *Whew, all my hard work and dedication paid off and got me a medal!* The silver medalists' story may have sounded like this: *Damn it, all that hard work, and I missed out on gold.*

Because of a more positive story, the gold and bronze medal winners felt more pride, joy, and gratitude, emotions reflected in their smiles. But the negative story of the silver medal winners caused them to feel more sadness, anger, frustration, and disappointment. And here's the crazy thing: Objectively speaking, the silver medalists did better than the bronze medalists, but they thought themselves into feeling worse.

---

* V.H. Medvec et al., "When Less Is More: Counterfactual Thinking and Satisfaction Among Olympic Medalists," *Journal of Personality and Social Psychology* 69, no. 4 (1995): 603–10, https://doi.org/10.1037/0022-3514.69.4.603.

What are the silver medals in your life—the things that are good or even great, but because they're not perfect, you talk yourself into feeling bad about them? No judgment: We all do this at times, and this pattern of thinking is even more common among former athletes, high achievers, and nerds (said affectionately by the nerdy, ambitious former athlete). When you tell yourself you need to be perfect and win gold every time in order to be happy, you're setting yourself up to experience more negative emotions.

A positive story leads to positive emotions, and a negative story leads to negative ones. You can have a perfect life and be miserable, or you can have a challenging life and be joyful—because a lot of your joy and happiness comes from your story.

What's the Story? Good or Bad

The two most powerful words in any story are "good" and "bad." Your opinions affect your emotions and behavior: If you label something as good, you'll be drawn to it—and if you experience that perceived goodness, you'll feel a positive emotion. On the other hand, if you label something as bad, you'll try to avoid it—and if you can't avoid it, you'll feel a negative emotion.

For instance, winter is just a natural part of life. It's not trying to hurt anybody. However, if your opinion is that winter sucks, you'll feel negative emotions anytime that season comes. Sometimes, our stories can trap us in a cycle of depression and anxiety. If we hate something that we can't avoid, we're emotionally stuck. And the thought of repeatedly facing something we hate can make us feel depressed or anxious.

Some things deserve a negative label, but if you put a negative label on everything, you'll be surrounded by things that fuel negative emotions. On the other hand, if you can up your optimism game and shift some of your stories to be more positive, then your joy, happiness, and peace will follow suit.

"I Am Responsible": A Crucial and Empowering Story

At age twenty-three, I listened to *The Psychology of Achievement* by Brian Tracy. I'm paraphrasing, but when he said something to the effect of "You are responsible for your success," I initially got defensive. I felt like he was blaming the victim. I thought to myself, *What about my boss, parents, and society?* He went on to say, "The first step to success is to stop blaming others and take responsibility." This was a valuable lesson, and I chose to embrace the story that I was responsible for my success and my emotions.

We often blame others for our stress and anxiety. But blaming is a disempowering story, because the power lies where the responsibility lies. If someone else is responsible for our feelings, then they have the power over how we feel—and we have to rely on them to feel good. In contrast, when we take responsibility for our feelings, we have the power to respond in any way we choose.

While we are individuals, we're also part of a whole. Belonging and safety are examples of psychosocial needs that partly rely on other people. So, our experience is connected to others, and the connection is what leads us to say others are making us feel a certain way. Ultimately, though, we create our emotions in our brains based on our concepts about life. We might think that other people are stressing us out and making us angry, but remember what Bonnie Raitt sang: Someone can't make you love them if you don't feel that way in your heart.

If someone can't make you love them, can they really "make" you angry, sad, happy, confident, or proud? We often say, "You made me so proud" or "They made me so angry," but it's more accurate to say, "You did something, and I made myself proud" or "That person did something, and I made myself angry." We're entitled to any emotion we choose, and sometimes anger is an appropriate response. But remember, we are the ones creating the feeling through our story, which means we have power.

A Lesson from the Big Apple

When my dad drove me from New Orleans to Boston for college, we stopped to visit my uncle in Brooklyn, New York. This was before GPS and smartphones, so all I had to get there was a paper map. And let's just say that driving in NYC is way different from driving in Louisiana. People were speeding and swerving, and Dad and I were freaking out.

We felt anxious because our need for safety wasn't being met. Our concept of safe and acceptable driving was different from New Yorkers'. We could blame the other drivers for making us feel anxious, but it was our own way of thinking that led to our emotions. At one point, I remember my dad shifting his concept of what was acceptable. He looked at me and said, "When in Rome..." Then, he hit the gas and started swerving himself.

We develop concepts of social norms, and those concepts influence how we experience people and events. We learn to be fearful in certain situations and joyful in others. When certain things happen, we learn to be angry or to be sad. Now, I'm not suggesting that you never feel anger or sadness; I just want you to feel empowered knowing you get to define what makes you angry or sad. You get to choose your story and your focus, and because of this power, you can work to develop a mindset that generates more joy and peace.

The Anatomy of **THINKING**: Mindset

Purposeful Mind (Conscious)	Focus	Story
Habit Mind (Subconscious)	Focus	Story

The Purposeful (Conscious) Mind
and the Habit (Subconscious) Mind

There are two layers to your thinking: a purposeful or conscious layer and a habit or subconscious layer. Through all your senses combined, your brain takes in 11 million bits of information *each second*, but you can only consciously process forty to fifty of them. To help process massive amounts of data, your brain creates thinking shortcuts—habits—and

95 percent of your thinking happens subconsciously, outside your awareness.

The Habit Loop: Cue → Behavior → Reward

The job of your subconscious mind is to run your life on auto-pilot, and you have a built-in reward-based learning system to help your brain do just that. Imagine one of your ancestors was roaming the savanna and stumbled upon a tree with a big, red fruit. After picking the fruit and tasting its amazing flavor, their brain would say to itself, *Remember what this is and where to find it.* And that's how the habit is born. Cue: big, red fruit. Behavior: picking and eating. Reward: tasty sugar high.

When you have a pleasant experience, a behavior gets filed in a "Yes, please, more of that" habit loop. But all rewards are not the addition of a positive experience; some are the avoidance of a negative experience. I used to love pad thai, but I got food poisoning one time and haven't had it in over twenty years. When you have an unpleasant experience, that behavior or situation will get filed in the "heck no, never again" habit part of the brain.

People usually think about habits in reference to behavior, but you also develop emotional habits because your subconscious thinking affects your emotional reactions. It could be one major event or repeatedly telling yourself the same story over and over that files something into the positive or negative category—but once a belief is established and put on autopilot, your emotions and behavior will become automatic, subconscious reflexes of that belief. Subconscious negativity leads to reflexive negative emotions.

Reacting vs. Responding

One of the differences between the conscious and subconscious mind is their processing speed. Your subconscious mind is fast, instinctive, and predictive like autosuggestion. It relies on past learning to regulate your body, emotions, and behavior automatically. Imagine you developed a fear of spiders after being bitten. Spiders would get filed in the "heck no" habit part of the brain. If someone came into the room and said they saw a spider, your heart rate and anxiety would instantly increase before you even knew any other details, thanks to your subconscious mind.

By contrast, your conscious mind is slower, more deliberate, and more creative. It uses past information, but it can also use logic and reasoning to consider alternative possibilities. Continuing with the spider example, if someone said they saw a spider, your conscious mind might pause and think, *The spider is in a different room, so there's no need to worry right now.*

This is the difference between reacting and responding. You need both automatic and purposeful thinking. Habits create efficiency; if you had to learn how to walk each day and consciously focus on every step, you'd never get anywhere. However, when your overall beliefs, stories, and mindset are more negative, you'll react negatively and habitually experience more negative emotions.

The good news is you can reprogram your subconscious mind to be more positive by purposefully updating some of your stories and intentionally practicing optimism. This is the essence of Mind Care. By consciously exercising your

Optimism Muscles, you can build positive thinking habits that lead to positive emotions.

Optimism Muscles That Create
Joy, Happiness, and Peace

All of your Optimism Muscles help create positive emotions, but your three core Optimism Muscles are (1) gratitude, focusing on the good in life; (2) self-appreciation, focusing on the good in yourself; and (3) appreciation of others, focusing on the good in others. In Part 2, we'll talk more about how to build up these thinking patterns, because when you strengthen your ability to focus on the good in life, self, and others, you'll experience more joy, happiness, and peace.

If you feel like you've always been more of a negative person, don't fret. We're all wired with a negativity bias to help us survive, and when we feed and exercise the negativity muscles, they grow bigger and stronger. But your positivity muscles can also grow!

When you start lifting weights, training for a marathon, or practicing yoga, you know it'll take time for your body to improve. Likewise, a change in mindset won't happen overnight. It takes mindfulness and repetition to strengthen your mindset, and I'm confident you can up your optimism game regardless of your starting point.

It also takes motivation to get started and keep going on any change that leads to more joy and peace. Luckily, in the next chapter, you'll learn how to use optimism to fuel your motivation.

 UP YOUR OPTIMISM GAME: COACH'S CORNER 

You may be motivated to up your optimism game so that you feel more joy, but there is extra power in your focus and story because as you become more joyful, confident, and peaceful, your positive presence will impact those around you. This is known as a ripple effect.

"Be the change you wish to see," and the positivity ripple will spread to family, friends, and colleagues. You can be a bright light and inspiration for others. But in order to be the light, you first have to *see* the light. So, practice looking for the good in life, self, and others, and you'll start shining a little brighter. Do it for yourself... and the world.

THREE

THE ANATOMY OF MOTIVATION

"The secret of getting ahead is getting started."
—UNKNOWN

JOE WANTED TO LOSE WEIGHT BUT HAD BEEN STRUG-gling to find his motivation to exercise. Here's what he said in our first coaching conversation:

I want to exercise more, but as I've gotten older, everything gets harder. A few years ago, I had surgery on my left knee, and now my right knee is acting up. My back and shoulder are also a little wonky from old football injuries, so that sometimes limits what I can do. I have a gym membership but never go. I've thought about trying to get back into running, but I don't think my knees will let me. I never can seem to stick to a diet, and there is so much on my plate at work.

My blood pressure is creeping up, and I'm worried if I keep gaining weight, I'll need medication.

If you want to feel more energy and vitality by changing your eating, exercise, and health habits, you need vision to start and determination to stay the course. And to inject more meaning and purpose into your life, you need the drive to pursue your passions, nurture your relationships, and contribute. Finally, to feel more accomplished and fulfilled by switching careers, writing a book, or starting a side hustle, you need the courage to take the first step.

Some of your joy, happiness, and peace is tied to your behavior. Whether it's a health, relationship, or career goal, you need motivation to build a life that fills you with positive emotions. And here's the biggest no-brainer statement about motivation: If you don't believe you can be successful, you won't even try in the first place. Optimism is a key ingredient in motivation because it breeds hope, confidence, and perseverance, which get you started and keep you going.

Motivation and emotion are related concepts that come from the same Latin root meaning "to move." To live your best life, you must tap into what moves you forward. With optimism, you can turn fear into faith, self-doubt into courage, and stuckness into action. Thinking plays a large role in the transformation, but first, let's look at the full anatomy of motivation.

Motivation is the driving force behind your actions, and it's influenced by what's happening in your body, your life, and your mind. In each area there are drives (accelerators) that push you forward and barriers (brakes) that slow you down or stop you. You'll act when the sum of your drives is higher than the sum of your barriers.

The Anatomy of **MOTIVATION**

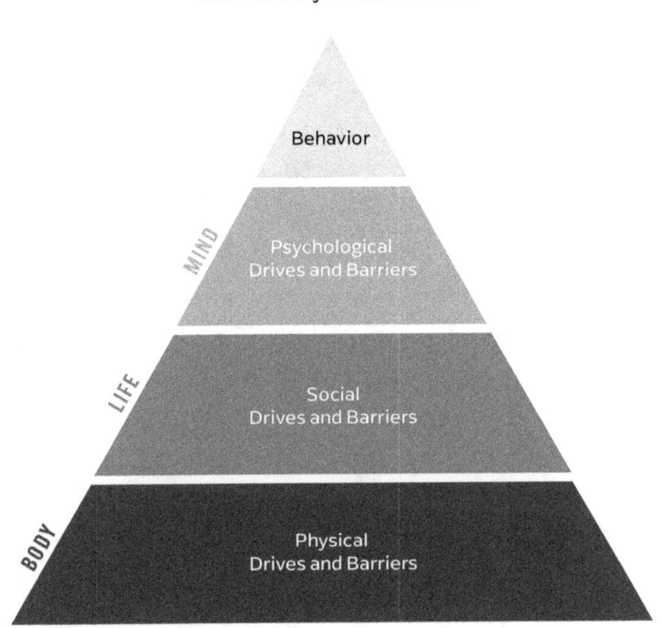

Drives (Accelerators)

Drives help you get your needs met. You have physical, social, and psychological needs, so you have physical, social, and psychological drives.

Physical (Biological) Drives

Some of your behavior is driven by your body. When you're hungry, thirsty, or tired, you eat, drink, or sleep. And if you're physically addicted to a substance, you'll be driven to consume it. Remember, your brain evolved to regulate your body, so your brain will push you to act in ways that serve physical needs.

Social Drives

In society, there are rewards for conforming to the norms and punishments for going against the grain. We work to earn money and try not to get fired. Also, as members of a team, tribe, or family, we are driven to protect or nurture our relationships.

Psychological Drives

We all have unique hopes, fears, values, and interests. If you love dancing, you might regularly attend dance classes, and if you hate clowns, you might avoid the circus. Dreams and fears drive behavior.

Competing Drives

Sometimes, we feel stuck because we have competing drives that pull us in different directions. We really want to go to our niece's soccer game, but we're way behind on work. We're tired and should sleep, but we're having so much fun playing games with our friends. We really want to put ourselves out there, but we also want to stay safe. One drive can be a barrier to change for a competing drive, and we may also get stopped by physical, social, and psychological barriers.

Barriers (Brakes)

Barriers are anything that make performing a behavior more challenging. You can be slowed down by your body, life, or mind.

Physical Barriers

Blood sugar is a strong predictor of willpower. If your energy is low or you have pain, that can prevent you from acting. Your confidence, courage, and motivation will be highest when you're pain-free and full of energy.

Social Barriers

Lacking resources—like time, money, support, or access—is one of the major social barriers. Psychologically, you might want to go to the gym, but if you don't have enough time or support, you won't add a gym routine.

Psychological Barriers

Common psychological barriers are importance, lack of knowledge or confidence, and fear. Obviously, if something isn't high on your priority and values list, you'll have less motivation to do it. And fear and doubt often stop us dead in our tracks.

Physical and social barriers are a natural part of life, but if you can overcome the psychological barriers, you can generate the motivation to take a positive step. This is where an optimistic mindset comes in.

Mindset and Motivation

All behavior is motivated by one of two forces: (1) approach or (2) avoid. You approach what is pleasant and enjoyable, and you avoid what is unpleasant and painful. You pursue hopes and dreams, and you avoid fears and worries. You act to grow and expand, or you act to protect and conserve.

Negativity and pessimism characterize the underlying mindset of avoidance. "Stay back," "Don't try," "Don't trust," and "Don't risk" are all negative thinking patterns designed to protect you and keep you safe. And while not trying protects you from failing, it also stops you from growing. In order to grow, you need to tap into optimism and positivity.

Focus and Motivation

At the beginning of this chapter, when Joe talked about his struggles with motivation, did you pick up on his focus? He spent five minutes telling me about his problems, limitations, failures, obstacles, and fears. All the negativity was causing him to avoid trying.

Questions direct focus, so in responding to him, I leaned on *appreciative inquiry*, or positive questions. I asked him, "In addition to losing weight, how do you hope your life will improve if you start exercising?"

He responded, "I hope my knees get stronger, so I'll have less pain. And I want more energy to do things outside of work. I also hope my blood pressure will stay normal, and I want to be a good role model to my teenage son."

Just this one positive question shifted his focus to his hopes and dreams, and he could feel his motivation increasing.

Focusing on negative aspects of change leads to avoiding the change. But focusing on the pros of changing increases your motivation to go after a goal. Also, when you focus on the negative aspects of yourself, you'll have less confidence. Self-appreciation is a core Optimism Muscle, and when you focus on the positive aspects of yourself, you'll have more confidence.

Finding Your Spark

Let's test out how positive questions can help you find a spark. To start, I want you to think about some change you're hoping to make in your life. Alright, got a goal in mind? Great. Now, answer these questions:

- If you could be successful in making this change, how do you hope your life would improve?
- What makes that vision meaningful and important to you?

Now, I want you to think back on something that you're proud to have accomplished:

- What does that story show you about your strengths and character?
- As you consider this new goal, what personal strengths can you lean on to be successful?
- In addition to your own strengths, who can you lean on for support?
- Imagine you're successful in reaching your goal. How does it feel?

After thinking about the answers to all those positive questions, did you notice an uptick in your motivation? In order to pursue growth, you need emotions like hope, faith, and confidence, which you can access through a positive focus. So, to increase your motivation, focus more on your hopes, dreams, vision, values, strengths, abilities, past successes, resources, and support.

Story and Motivation

Imagine two forty-five-year-olds, who both find out they are prediabetic. That weekend, they both decide to get back in shape by going for a run. They haven't run in years, so you know how this is going to go. They start to jog, and thirty seconds in, their lungs are burning, their hearts are racing, and their knees are aching. At this point, they have to tell themselves a story about what's going on.

The first person thinks, *Man, I'm old and out of shape. My running days are behind me. I guess diabetes is part of getting older.* The second person thinks, *Man, I'm old and out of shape. I have to keep at it to build myself back up and prevent diabetes for as long as I can.*

These are two people with similar situations, but the stories they tell themselves lead them down different paths. The person with the pessimistic story is likely to feel anxious about their health, depressed by their situation, and ultimately like they should give up. On the other hand, the person with the optimistic story is likely to feel empowered, hopeful, and excited about the pursuit of a goal to make their life better.

Negative stories will crush your motivation: *I suck, I'm lazy, I can't do it, I'm a failure, I'm not worthy, I can't change, I'm too old, and I'm not good enough.* But positive stories will fire you up! Imagine telling yourself stories like these: *I love myself, I'm a hard worker, I can do it, I'm a winner, I am worthy, I can learn, I can grow, I can change, others have done it and so can I, I have strengths, I have talents, I have choices, and I have power.*

In Chapter 2, I mentioned that subconscious negativity can lead to reflexive negative emotions. Well, another challenge with unconscious negativity is reflexive avoidant behavior or procrastination. If you have deep-seated fears or negative beliefs, procrastination is a great way to avoid the prospect of a negative experience. So, you may feel stuck going after your goals because of negative self-limiting beliefs. By contrast, when you have deep-seated faith, confidence, and hope, you'll reflexively go after your goals and behave in ways that lead to success.

Whatever your goal, your stories will influence your drive. Optimism starts an upward spiral. Positive thoughts make you feel good emotionally, and that positive emotional state gives you motivation to change. You feel good, so you *do* good. And when you do good, you *feel* good—perpetuating a positive cycle.

Optimism Muscles That Build Motivation

There are multiple ways to get motivated. Twelve Optimism Muscles that can help increase motivation are vision, mindfulness, dreaming, hope, faith, confidence, courage, meaning, passion, agency, self-appreciation, and self-compassion.

You don't have to focus on strengthening all of them at the same time. Depending on your situation, a little vision, hope, or dreaming might do the trick to unlock your motivation. Or maybe you just need confidence and faith in yourself.

If you've been trained your whole life to look for problems, weaknesses, and reasons why something won't work for you, it may take some time to up this part of your optimism game. But you can start by asking yourself one positive question over and over: *What if it works?*

New job, new relationship, new health and fitness routine: What if it works? What if they say yes? What if it works out even better than imagined?

It's okay to ask, "What if it doesn't work?" That's a protective question. But "What if it works?" is a growth question that keeps you focused on hopes, dreams, and positive outcomes. And even if it doesn't "work," life is a journey filled with lessons and adventures. And what if it does work?!

Hopefully, you're starting to understand your inner emotional anatomy. Focus and story affect feelings, and feelings affect actions. So, you can use your thinking to fuel your motivation to do things that generate joy, happiness, and peace.

We've covered the anatomy of emotions, thinking, and motivation, so in the next chapter...let's talk about stress, baby.

 UP YOUR OPTIMISM GAME: COACH'S CORNER 

A lot of your motivation is in your focus:

Negative Focus to Avoid Change	*Positive Focus to Pursue Change*
Fear and Worries	*Hopes and Dreams*
Others' Visions and Values	*Your Vision and Values*
Weaknesses and Limitations	*Strengths and Abilities*
Past Failures	*Past Successes*
Obstacles and Barriers	*Resources and Support*

If there's a goal you're trying to get motivated to pursue, check your focus.

Are you focusing on a negative aspect of changing, like obstacles and fears? And are you focusing on some negative aspect of yourself, like your weaknesses and past failures?

If so, try using positive questions to help shift your focus to your resources, hopes, strengths, and past successes.

Your hopes and dreams are possible. You have strengths and abilities. You got this!

FOUR

THE ANATOMY OF STRESS

*"The greatest weapon against stress is our
ability to choose one thought over another."*
—WILLIAM JAMES

D O YOU THINK STRESS IS BAD FOR YOU OR GOOD for you?

A 1998 survey asked thirty thousand participants two questions:

- Did you experience a large amount of stress last year?
- Do you think stress is harmful to your health?

Years later, researchers reviewed the death records and found that people who experienced a large amount of stress and believed stress was harmful were 43 percent more likely to have died. However, the group with the lowest death rates were people who experienced a lot of stress but didn't believe stress was harmful. This led the researchers to conclude that the perception that stress is harmful likely contributed to excess deaths.*

For years, I believed stress was only bad and encouraged clients to avoid it like the plague, but after reading *The Upside of Stress* by Dr. Kelly McGonigal, my mindset toward stress changed. As we explore the anatomy of stress, I invite you to rethink your stress mindset as well.

Circumstances vs. Perception

Four main factors influence your experience of stress: your situation, behavior, body, and mind. If you can change a difficult situation through behavior, that's a good place to start. Leaving a job that's not a good fit or ending a bad relationship can decrease your stress. But some situations are not easily changeable. Most people can't quit working or fire their kids, so working and caregiving are likely things that you're stuck with.

When faced with "stressful" circumstances that aren't easily changeable, you can increase Body Care activities, like exercise and sleep, to increase your resilience to stress. But often the best way to transform your experience of stress is through your mind.

In her book *The How of Happiness*, happiness researcher Sonja Lyubomirsky explains that 10 percent of our happiness comes from our circumstances, whereas 40 percent comes

---

* Abiola Keller et al., "Does the Perception That Stress Affects Health Matter? The Association with Health and Mortality," *Health Psychology* 31, no. 5 (Sept. 2012): 677–84, https://doi.org/10.1037/a0026743.

from voluntary elements like thoughts and actions. Many people struggle to handle stress when they overvalue the role their situation plays over their emotions and spend all their time trying to change everything around them instead of looking inward.

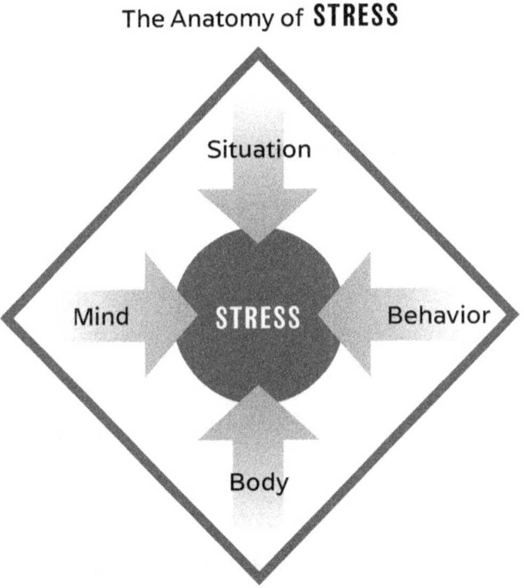

Your story is a powerful stress-transformation tool. And if you change your mindset about three things—stress itself, your situation, and life—you can go from anxious, overwhelmed, and burned out to energized, encouraged, calm, or at peace.

Stories About Stress

To understand how our perception of stress affects our health, let's talk about the placebo and nocebo effects. Placebo derives from the Latin word meaning "to please." The placebo effect occurs when someone gets a fake treatment, but because they think something good will happen, their problem improves. Sometimes when people are given sugar pills and told it's pain medicine, they have a reduction in pain, because what we believe influences how our body responds. Positive expectations can support healing.

Nocebo derives from the Latin word meaning "to harm." The nocebo effect occurs when someone develops symptoms because they think something bad will happen. A lumbar puncture (spinal tap) is a routine diagnostic tool, and one potential side effect of this test is a headache. In one study, seven out of fifteen patients who were warned they might get a headache after their spinal tap reported getting one, whereas only one out of thirteen patients who were not warned reported a headache.* Think about that: Nearly half of patients suffered from a headache only when they were warned about potential danger.

Results like these have started an ethical debate in health care about informed consent. If the goal is to do no harm, how much potential harm is being caused by always "warning" people that negative things can happen? Negative expectations can lead to sickness.

Stress Is Bad...Right?

It's true that stress can potentially cause negative effects on your body, mind, and behavior—headaches, muscle tension,

---

* A.M. Daniels and R. Sallie, "Headache, Lumbar Puncture, and Expectation," *The Lancet* 317, no. 8227 (May 1981): 1003, https://doi.org/10.1016/s0140-6736(81)91771-2.

fatigue, sleep problems, anxiety, depression, and more. And stress can drive you to overeat, smoke, misuse drugs and alcohol, or socially isolate.

As a society, we've developed a completely pessimistic view about stress, yet some of our worries are overblown because of a misuse of the word. Much of the early research on stress was conducted on rats, and when rats are stressed out by researchers, they experience lots of negative changes. But what gets left out is that attempts to "stress out" rats amount to torture.

To study the stress response, researchers have made rats tread water until they nearly drowned, confined them to cages so they couldn't move, and exposed them to bigger rats that would bully them. Being stuck in a cage with someone who is bullying you is a wholly different situation from being stuck in traffic. But with headlines like "Research Shows Stress Is Killing You," it's easy to see why people get freaked out about "stress."

Of course, stressful and traumatic events can have negative effects on you. Post-traumatic stress disorder (PTSD) is real—but so is post-traumatic growth. And studies have shown that the majority of people who experience trauma or challenging life situations report growth.

This is not meant to shame or demean anyone who suffers, and the fact that there is growth doesn't mean there is no suffering or pain. But it can be useful to see the other side of the stress story. Can you think of a time when you went through something hard and it made you a stronger and better person?

If you have a completely negative view of stress, you're going to have negative physical and emotional responses to it. So, it's useful to understand the upside of stress too.

Stress Is Good!

In addition to helping you grow, stress can give you energy, help you focus, improve performance, strengthen relationships, and help you rise to meet challenges. Remember, pressure makes diamonds.

One of your positive stress responses is called "excite and delight." It leads to the exhilarating feeling you get when kissing someone, skydiving, cheering for a sports team, singing at a concert, or playing interesting and challenging games.

Another positive stress response is called "tend and befriend." Stress can kick in your social instincts and increase your tendency to connect, serve, protect, and support others. Think of mama bears and social butterflies.

Also, your stress response can protect you from PTSD. Maybe you've heard that cortisol, a major stress hormone, is bad. However, in a study of accident victims, researchers found that the higher the cortisol level following a traumatic accident, the lower the chance the person would have flashbacks and PTSD.* A popular narrative is that cortisol is harming you, but it's often helping you!

But wait, stress has to be bad...right? Researchers surveyed people from over one hundred countries to see if the level of stress in a country could predict measures of well-being. They found that countries with the highest levels of stress also had the highest levels of life satisfaction. Yep, you heard me right.

---

* D.L. Delahanty et al., "Initial Posttraumatic Urinary Cortisol Levels Predict Subsequent PTSD Symptoms in Motor Vehicle Accident Victims," *Biological Psychiatry* 48, no. 9 (Nov. 2000): 940–47, https://doi.org/10.1016/s0006-3223(00)00896-9.

McGonigal refers to this as the "stress paradox." You feel stress when something you care about is at stake. A meaningful life is inherently a stressful life, because the more things you have to care about, the more things will cause you "stress."

If you think about the things that cause you the most stress, the list likely includes your kids, partner, parents, job, or home. But would you give them up? Interestingly, some studies show that trying to avoid stress actually increases depression. When you try to avoid stress, you inadvertently decrease how much meaning is in your life.

You don't want to deal with the stress of driving your toddler to Grandma's, so you stay a little more isolated. You don't want to deal with the stress of posting on social media, so you never chase your dream and start your side gig. If you embrace the idea that stress can be useful, you'll stop trying to avoid life and instead truly engage in and live life.

In fact, rather than saying you have stress, I think it's more useful to say you have *life*. And you don't just experience life; you experience your *stories* about life. Your beliefs and expectations color your reality. By adopting a more optimistic mindset toward stress, you can change how you physically and mentally experience it.

Stories About Situations

Changing how you view a situation can change your experience of stress, anxiety, fatigue, and burnout. There are three key shifts in story that can help you make that transformation.

Stress and Anxiety: From Threat to Challenge

One of Kristen's biggest emotional challenges was anxiety. I explained to her that when she viewed something as a threat, she'd feel anxious, worried, or fearful, and the negative lens would lead her to avoid or procrastinate. However, if she chose to view something as a challenge, she'd be more likely to feel energized, focused, and determined.

Sometimes, labeling something as a threat is the most appropriate response. But if you go around labeling everything as bad, dangerous, and threatening, you'll live in a constant state of anxiety. You can transform your experience of stress and anxiety by recrafting some of your stories of threat into stories of challenge.

Optimistic Leadership: Decatastrophizing

During my early days as a health professional, I probably caused a lot of anxiety in my patients by cautioning them about everything. *Don't let your knees go over your toes, don't press overhead, don't arch your back*—all of those things might cause pain.

As a leader, my pessimistic voice took over, and I constantly tried to protect people by warning them about what to avoid. Then, a couple years into coaching, I had a weird epiphany. I noticed that many clients were anxious about food. And the origin of their anxiety was the belief that certain foods were threatening.

Doctors have said eggs, butter, and red meat will kill you. Sugar is toxic. Too much fat, too much protein, or too many carbs will kill you. Pesticides on fruits and veggies will kill you. GMOs, high-fructose corn syrup, artificial flavors, artificial colors, sugar substitutes, and any processed food will kill you. Well, damn, what am I supposed to eat?

In an unintentional way, the advancement of medical knowledge has contributed to the rise in anxiety. To prevent people from dying, we spend millions of dollars studying what will do harm, and then we scream through public health campaigns warning people at every turn. But if you pathologize everything about life, no place is safe, and that perception is a recipe for constant anxiety.

This overprotective instinct doesn't just happen in medicine. As a leader, parent, or helping professional, your focus and story will influence the emotions of the people you lead. If you only lead with pessimism and try to motivate by fear, it will add to the anxiety of the people you're trying to help.

The solution? As I said in Chapter 1, decatastrophize and reframe. If you tend to think of the worst-case scenario, you can decatastrophize by first thinking about the best-case scenario and then the most likely scenario. Having best-case and likely scenarios in mind makes the overall picture less negative and can decrease worry and anxiety.

Stress and Fatigue: From "Have To" to "Get To"

"Have to" and "get to" are two little expressions that make a big difference in your experience of stress. A sense of autonomy and freedom is energizing, but when you feel like you're being forced into something, it can drain the life out of you. "Have to" evokes a sense of obligation and dread, which will weigh you down emotionally and sap your energy: *I have to go to work. I have to exercise. I have to help my parents.*

But changing one word can completely flip the script: *I get to go to work. I get to exercise. I get to help my parents.* Many of my friends have lost their parents, but I'm still blessed. I still get to live out my own values of love and kindness by helping two of the most important people in my life. "Get to" is an empowering story that evokes a spirit of choice and opportunity, and it can create feelings of excitement, anticipation, and gratitude.

If you live your entire life through the lens of obligation, life will feel heavy and exhausting. But if you can shift some of your "have tos" into "get tos," you'll feel lighter, more energetic, and eager to face each new day.

Stress and Burnout: From Meaningless to Meaningful

At the University of Rochester, physicians participated in a study on burnout and mental health. In the beginning, their average score on a depression and anxiety survey was 33, which signals high levels of mental distress. For comparison, in the general population, women score around 20 and men around 15.*

The study then provided an intervention program that did two things. Each session began with mindfulness and breathing exercises, and then participants practiced talking differently about their jobs. Instead of focusing on all the negative elements of their work, they focused on meaning and contribution. The physicians asked each other questions like "What

---

* Michael S. Krasner et al., "Association of an Educational Program in Mindful Communication with Burnout, Empathy, and Attitudes Among Primary Care Physicians," *JAMA* 302, no. 12 (Sept. 2009): 1284–93, https://doi.org/10.1001/jama.2009.1384.

made that interaction meaningful and memorable?" or "In the face of a challenge, what did you do to ease suffering or make a positive difference?"

After two months of this program, the average score was down to 15, and after a year, the average was down to 11. The physicians went from feeling extremely burned out and emotionally distressed to reporting higher levels of work satisfaction, connection with patients, and emotional well-being—without changing anything about their situation. By shifting how they thought and talked about work, they changed their *experience* of work.

Without meaning, hard work feels like nothing but suffering that beats you down. But when you can connect your effort to something meaningful, the experience can lift you up. Can you think of instances where you poured blood, sweat, and tears into something that energized you? Maybe it was training for a sport, mastering an art form, getting a degree, or raising kids. If the hard work is "worth it," most of us will gladly do it.

Meaning and purpose unlock your energy, courage, determination, love, contribution, and gratitude. If there is a stressful situation that is leading you to feel burned out, look for meaning. Remember your values. Identify your contribution.

Stories About Life

We develop beliefs and philosophies about life from family, society, and our own experiences. And our mindset toward aspects of life like success and relationships will influence our feelings of stress, anxiety, overwhelm, and burnout.

Success: Do Everything, Know Everything, Fix Everything

One incident that had a big impact on my mindset toward success was the Junior Pledge Ceremony for Sargent College at Boston University. Junior Pledge is when all the allied health students pledge their commitment to excellence as they move from preprofessional curriculum to specialized professional curriculum.

During my ceremony, when awards were given to students for extracurricular activities and service to the college, not a single one went to a physical therapy student. Feeling left out, I turned to my friend and said, "It's easy for them to do extracurricular activities, because their schedule isn't as jam-packed as ours."

While back in New Orleans for the summer, I wrestled with the idea that I wasn't enough and considered adding more things to my plate—even though I was already stretched thin. My jealousy and ego kept nudging me to do more so that I could be recognized. Then one day, I was driving down Franklin Avenue in the Ninth Ward in my Dodge Shadow, and I yelled out the window, "F it—I'm going to do it all!" (But I said something stronger than "F it.")

When senior year started, I was a man on a mission, and I participated in more than ten extracurriculars in the first semester alone. I was on the track team and sang in the gospel choir. I attended meetings for the Black Student Union and the National Science Foundation. I had a job at the school gym and a job tutoring kids in the inner city. I was a peer counselor and became the senior class representative. If someone asked me to do it, I said, "YES!" And halfway through the fall semester, I had my first bout with insomnia. I slept less than four hours a night for about five weeks. I had so much to do and think about that it was difficult to turn off my brain, and I couldn't take time off, because people were counting on me.

I jumped from thing to thing, pouring my heart and soul into each role, and you know what? All my striving paid off. That year, I made the dean's list and graduated magna cum laude. And I won three awards, including the Bernard Kutner Award, the highest honor given to a graduating senior at Sargent College. I felt so validated and proud, and my addiction to doing everything was born.

Sometimes, we attempt to do everything because we seek love, acceptance, and validation from others or ourselves. Three Optimism Muscles that can help with this sense of lack are self-appreciation, self-love, and confidence. When you get better at loving yourself and appreciating your contribution, you can feel you are enough, so you don't have to constantly attempt to validate your worth through endless achievement.

Now, don't get me wrong: Doing things can be fun and rewarding, and achievement can lead to emotions like joy, pride, and fulfillment. So, I'm not saying that you shouldn't do anything, but just like you can eat too much chocolate, you can also do too much.

As a nerdy, athletic high achiever and recovering perfectionist, I can identify with people who do so many things that they feel burned out all the time. The drive to be successful, smart, and fit can easily turn into an obsession that disregards your physical, emotional, or social needs. And once the achievement pattern of thinking gets locked in place, it can sometimes drive you into the ground.

To decrease overwhelm and burnout, strike a balance between striving to do more and simply resting and accepting. When navigating the "strive versus rest" line, you can use your vision muscles (more on this in Chapter 10) to define your boundaries and priorities so that you feel less pressure to do everything and can focus on what matters most. Growth is good, but you don't have to do everything, say yes to everything, and be good at everything.

Letting Go of Knowing Everything

It's easy to get overwhelmed and develop analysis paralysis when you're obsessed with trying to know everything, be "perfect," or find the best way to do something. When answering a question like "What's the best way to lose weight?" you can drive yourself crazy by going down the endless wormhole of thinking.

How often should I do weights, how heavy, how many sets, how many reps? How should I eat—vegan, keto, intermittent fasting, intuitive eating? And what about cardio—how much, how often, what type? And on and on you can go. It's easy to overthink, because life's possibilities are infinite and thinking is infinite. You can always ask one more question, and if you're desperate to know exactly how everything works, you'll endlessly chase your tail and exhaust yourself mentally and physically.

Practice letting go of the need to know everything. Use the knowledge you have, act on faith, take a step, and learn from your experience. When someone asks a random question, simply say, "I don't know"—and then let it go, instead of speculating endlessly about what the answer could be. If you forget something when with friends, resist the tendency to take out your phone to look it up. Practice being okay with forgetting some things.

Curiosity is cool, and learning feels good. But you don't need to understand, figure out, remember, and know everything.

Letting Go of Fixing Everything

Problem-solving is part of our nature, and fixing things feels good because (1) it's inherently rewarding to use our skills and abilities to solve problems, and (2) contribution is meaningful. Service is a behavior that's linked to high levels of emotional well-being. If you can help a child, patient, customer, or organization by fixing something, it makes sense that you will be drawn to doing so. And since humans are imperfect, you'll never run out of things to fix.

Practice noticing an imperfection and letting it stand. When you see something that could be fixed, pause, take a breath, and ask yourself, *Is this urgent, important, and necessary?* If so, act on it; if not, try letting it go. In addition, if a negative story is creating worry and compelling you to fix something, think about the best-case and most likely scenarios if you let the imperfection stand, which may help take off the edge. Fixing is fun, but you don't have to fix everything.

It can be hard to admit that your mindset toward life is burning you out. But if you think you have to do, know, and fix everything, you'll burn the candle at both ends—and then overwhelm, anxiety, and exhaustion are inevitable. However, you can work to shift your mindset about life to experience more serenity, peace of mind, and ease.

Relationships: Taming the Urge to Control and Fix Everyone

The movie *Finding Nemo* can teach us a lot about how our mindset toward relationships affects our stress and anxiety. If you haven't seen the movie, Marlin is an anxious and overprotective single-dad clown fish, and his son Nemo has a smaller fin on one side. Marlin worries so much about his son that he tries to control everything Nemo does, and when Nemo rebels and leaves the "safe zone," he gets taken by a scuba diver.

While searching for Nemo, Marlin tells Dory, "I promised him I'd never let anything happen to him." Dory replies, "That's a funny thing to promise. Well, you can't never let anything happen to him, then nothing would ever happen to him. Not much fun for little Harpo." At the end of the movie, Marlin realizes that he has to let go of trying to control Nemo and allow him the freedom to live his life on his own terms—and Nemo saves the day!

Compassionate Domination vs. Autonomy-Supportive

In *Finding Nemo*, Marlin's emotions go from anxiety to peace when he changes his leadership style from what I call *Compassionate Domination* to an *Autonomy-Supportive* style. I coined the term Compassionate Domination to describe what happens when someone cares so much about someone else that they try to dominate and control the other person, in an attempt to guarantee a positive outcome for them. But does anyone really feel cared for when they are being dominated?

Parents want the best for their kids, and sometimes they show their love and compassion by trying to dominate their child's life and control everything they do so that the child never makes mistakes or gets harmed in any way. In reality, we cannot truly control anyone, and trying to do so can be a source of anxiety, anger, and frustration in our relationships—for us and the other person.

Autonomy and freedom are among the strongest psychological drives. If you get better at supporting other people's autonomy, you will notice a huge positive shift in yourself, the other person, and the relationship. You will feel more at ease when you release responsibility to the other person, and they will feel unburdened and empowered. In addition, they'll feel respected and valued for their own opinions. Instead of wanting to run away from your control and domination, they will feel even more connected and drawn to you.

I know it's hard not to want to control everyone, because domination and control are the most common leadership styles we experience. Parents, grandparents, sports coaches, teachers, and bosses constantly tell us what to do, so it's tempting to do the same with others. However, the more control you seek over others, the more anxious or angry you'll be.

If you instead become more Autonomy-Supportive and strengthen Optimism Muscles like appreciation of others, faith, hope, agreeableness, serenity, and forgiveness, you'll experience more harmony and peace of mind.

Letting Go of Fixing Everyone

When I started coaching, I wanted to fix everyone and do everything in my power to make sure everyone reached their goals. For instance, a client once told me she had polycystic ovary syndrome (PCOS), and I promptly bought a book about PCOS so that I could help "fix" her.

This approach left me feeling exhausted and burned out, because every time someone came to see me, I obsessed over how to solve all their problems. Then one day, a coaching mentor said to me, "Charles, if you're working harder to fix the problem than your clients are, you're doing coaching wrong." She went on to say, "The client is responsible for the outcome, and it's your job to coach them, not to micromanage every aspect of their life."

This was a revelation to me as a helper and leader. Ultimately, everyone has to live their own life and choose their own path. And try as you might, you can't *make* anyone happy. They have to choose happiness for themselves.

If you can learn to let go of the desire to control everyone, you'll feel less anxious or angry and more at peace. And if you let go of the burden of trying to fix everyone and being responsible for everyone's happiness and success, you'll feel less overwhelmed and burned out.

Optimism Muscles That Transform Stress

Going back to the question that started this chapter, stress can be good or bad. When you're going through a tough, "stressful" time, I know you just want it to be over. Sometimes, you may have to sit patiently and embrace the idea that "this too shall pass." Sometimes, you have to summon the humility and courage to ask for help. And sometimes, you have to find the will to do something about the situation.

But remember, in addition to fueling your motivation to do something, your mindset is a powerful stress-management tool. How you think about life shapes your reality. Some Optimism Muscles that can help you transform your experience of stress are gratitude, self-appreciation, appreciation of others, vision, mindfulness, serenity, love, self-compassion, confidence, courage, meaning-making, agency, faith, and hope.

Again, you don't have to train every muscle at once; it just depends on your goals. Gratitude can decrease stress. Meaning-making at work can help with burnout. Faith can be an antidote to anxiety. With practice and the right Mindset Workout, you can train your brain to create more confidence, calm, peace, and serenity. And in Part 2, I'll teach you my method to build each muscle.

PART 1 SUMMARY: YOUR INNER WORLD ANATOMY

1. **The Anatomy of Emotion**: Emotions are created by the interplay between your mind, body, and behavior. Positive changes in any area lead to more positive emotions.

2. **The Anatomy of Thinking**: Mindset is a product of focus and story, both conscious and subconscious. Positive focus and positive story lead to more positive emotions.

3. **The Anatomy of Motivation**: Behavior is driven by physical, social, and psychological needs. Behavior is prevented by physical, social, and psychological barriers. A positive focus and story lead to higher levels of confidence and motivation to pursue growth.

4. **The Anatomy of Stress**: Your experience of stress is influenced by your situation, body, behavior, and mind. Positive stories and a positive stress mindset lead to a more positive experience of stress.

THE METHOD
BUILDING YOUR OPTIMISM

When I was eleven, I went to a basketball camp, and at the end, my dad bought two VHS videotapes from the instructor. One tape taught dribbling and passing, and the other taught shooting. The shooting tape used the acronym BEEF: **b**alance, **e**yes on the target, **e**lbow straight, **f**ollow through.

After watching the tape, I went to the backyard and missed a lot of shots. But I kept practicing BEEF for years and eventually became so skillful that I once made twenty-eight free throws in a row. Knowledge alone doesn't make you good at something, and stopping at knowledge is the reason many people don't get better. You can read books, watch videos, and attend lectures about shooting a basketball, but the only way to get more skillful is through practice.

The same is true of optimism. Knowing gratitude is good for you is one thing; regularly practicing it enough to become skillful at it is another. In addition to discussing your three core Optimism Muscles (gratitude, self-appreciation, and appreciation of others) and the four keys to effective optimism, in Part 2, I'm going to teach you my Think, Speak, Write Mindset Workout Method.

I developed this method to give you a simple yet effective way to train your brain. As you're working to become more optimistic, you're going to miss some shots. And even when you get good at optimism, you'll still experience negative emotions sometimes. But if you keep practicing, you'll become more skillful at generating joy, happiness, and peace.

FIVE

THE FOUR KEYS TO EFFECTIVE OPTIMISM

"There is a wisdom of the head,
and a wisdom of the heart."
—CHARLES DICKENS

BACK WHEN JOE WAS STILL REELING FROM HIS divorce, his best friend kept telling him to look on the bright side, but those conversations only made him angrier. So, when we started working together, Joe was skeptical about optimism.

"But Charles, I'm a realist," he told me. "I'm not going to turn into Pollyanna."

As an intellectual, he didn't believe it was smart or possible to be positive all the time. I agree. So, how much positivity do you need to feel good and thrive?

According to psychologist Barbara Fredrickson, who popularized the term *positivity ratio*, when people have three positive thoughts for every negative thought (a 3:1 ratio), they tend to show signs of mental wellness and emotional thriving. But when people have a ratio of one positive thought for every negative thought (a 1:1 ratio), they show signs of depression and languishing.

The great news is that in order to feel like you're thriving emotionally, you don't need total positivity; you just need slightly more positivity than negativity. Fredrickson also found that if people had a ratio of 1:1, they could boost it up to 3:1 or greater by formally practicing gratitude.

Gratitude is a powerful Optimism Muscle; however, practicing gratitude is just one way to increase your positivity. You have twenty-three additional Optimism Muscles, and strengthening any of them can improve your ratio.

Now, this is important: In order to feel good emotionally, you don't have to eliminate negative emotions from your mind. The ratio is not 3:0. Negative emotions are a natural and necessary part of life, so I'm not advising that you deny they exist. Instead, I encourage you to cultivate more optimism and positivity so that, despite the inevitable bumps in the road, you feel like you're thriving instead of just surviving.

Why Smart People Reject Cultivating Positivity

People often associate being realistic with being wise and grounded, and they think of positive thinking as unwise, delusional, and unrealistic. But if you dig into it, you'll notice optimism and pessimism can be equally wise or off base.

Thinking you'll win the lottery is slightly delusional, but by the same token, worrying you'll get attacked by a shark is also slightly delusional. Hopes and dreams are just like worries and fears. There's always a range of possibility.

Optimists and pessimists can both be realists, but they will have different experiences of life. If you mostly focus on real negative things, like crimes, you'll feel one way—and if you mostly focus on real positive things, like cherished relationships, you'll feel a different way.

The magic of thinking is in perception and imagination. If you mostly imagine negative things (apocalyptic futures), you'll feel negative emotions—and if you mostly imagine positive things (progress and prosperity), you'll feel positive emotions.

For centuries, pessimists have been predicting negative futures that never come to pass, yet because they explain their opinions with such eloquence and conviction, many people come to believe in those apocalyptic predictions—even when they're completely wrong. Pessimism and worry can be just as "delusional" as optimism.

Speaking of delusional, Barbara Fredrickson found that when someone had a positivity ratio of more than eleven positive thoughts for every negative thought (a ratio greater than 11:1), they tended to be delusional or out of touch. So, you *can* have too much positivity. But don't let a fear of delusion stop you from cultivating the wise kind of positivity.

You can be a smart, rational, optimistic realist, and because you'll experience more positive emotions than your pessimistic counterparts, optimism may actually be the wiser choice.

Mastering the Four Keys

For your optimism to be maximally effective, it should be (1) heartfelt and believable, (2) personally chosen, (3) used at the right time, and (4) in the right dose.

Key 1: Heartfelt and Believable

When practicing optimism, the thoughts you attempt to internalize must be heartfelt and believable to you. Many people think of putting a positive spin on life as denying what you actually feel and lying to yourself about what you believe. You don't have to lie to yourself to increase your positivity ratio, but you can shift your focus to good things that you believe are true. You can also recraft your stories to expand what you believe is true. The more heartfelt and believable a statement is, the more impact it will make.

Key 2: Personally Chosen

The second key is that you must personally choose to embrace the positive thought. You will have encouragers in your life who mean well when they point out positives. But sentiments have a more powerful effect when you are the one choosing them.

"You're a great mother." "You did really well during the meeting." "You look amazing." How often have you heard encouraging statements like these but just brushed them off because someone else said them? Even when encouragers say things you kinda believe, a statement will always have more impact if you have personally chosen to embrace it.

COACHING ACTION: CHOOSE YOUR OWN SILVER LININGS

Encouragers can also unwittingly make you reject positivity when they try to impose their positive spins on your suffering. You lost your job, and friends are telling you to look for the opportunity. Your family member is gravely ill, and people want you to think of all the good times. You just got hit by a freaking bus, and people want you to be grateful it wasn't worse.

These situations suck! So, anger, anxiety, or sadness are appropriate emotions to feel. And it can be frustrating when someone else seems to dismiss your suffering with a silver lining, even if the silver lining may technically be true. People who care about you just want to make you feel better. But you have the most powerful opinion, and what you personally choose to believe and focus on will have the biggest impact on your emotions. So, choose your own silver linings.

Key 3: Right Time

Walking is a great form of physical activity, but immediately after foot surgery isn't the best time to start a walking program. You have to let your foot heal first, and when you get the green light, you may need to take it slow.

When you suffer an emotional injury, hear bad news, or experience a loss, that moment might not be the best time to rush back to positivity. Recovery time depends on the severity of the injury, and often, honoring the negative emotion speeds up healing compared to engaging in denial. When you recognize that you are hurting, you can further enhance healing by sending love and kindness to yourself and asking for support. Then, when you're ready, use optimism to rehab your mindset.

Key 4: Right Dose

Medicine uses the terms *minimum effective dose* and *overdose*. If you only practice gratitude once a year, that's not a big enough dose to get a therapeutic effect. On the other hand, if you take too much positivity at once, it may be less effective. For example, if you made a mistake and are struggling with being your own worst critic, trying to embrace the affirmation "I am supremely confident in my ability" might be too huge of a positivity pill to swallow at the beginning. So, you might need a slightly smaller dose of positivity, like "I am learning to be more confident" or "I can grow, I can evolve, and I can change." Use the first key of heartfelt and believable as a dosing guide.

Choose Optimism

The journey to more joy, happiness, and peace starts with both a belief that cultivating positivity is good and a desire to up your optimism game. Some people will keep sharing all their reasons why positivity is bad. This is their negativity bias speaking. Some people will tell you why you should worry about everything. This is their attempt to protect you or others from harm. Some people will tell you to be realistic, when they really mean "Don't dream big" or "Don't get your hopes up."

This is their way of trying to protect you from disappointment and failure.

Sometimes, it's wise to heed the warnings. But there is wisdom of the heart, and you get to decide for yourself. *You* can choose growth or protection. *You* can choose joy or misery. *You* can choose hope or fear. *You* can choose optimism, and it can transform your mind, body, and soul. In the next chapter, we'll talk about how to exercise your mind so that you can reap the emotional health benefits of optimism.

 **UP YOUR OPTIMISM GAME: COACH'S CORNER** 

What do you want to believe is true? Earlier, I suggested trying to embrace positive thoughts that are believable, so you don't feel like you're lying to yourself. This is to support alignment with your current self-concepts.

But you can also align with future hopes, dreams, and aspirations, as long as they are heartfelt and reflect your deepest values and wishes. If you want to believe something is true, you have to practice that belief to *expand* your self-concepts. So, it's okay to try to swallow a big positivity pill, if you're willing and the dream is heartfelt.

SIX

THE MINDSET WORKOUT METHOD

*"Every day do something that will inch
you closer to a better tomorrow."*
—DOUG FIREBAUGH

AT THIS POINT, YOU MIGHT BE THINKING, *CHARLES, this all makes sense about how my thinking influences my emotions, but how do I train my brain to be less negative and more positive so that I actually feel more joy, happiness, and peace?*

I'm glad you asked. As a physical therapist and trainer, I recommended that my clients use some combination of strength training, cardio, and stretching to work out their bodies. As an optimism coach, I advise my clients to use some combination of thinking, speaking, and writing to work out their minds.

In exercise terms:

- Thinking = Strength Training
- Speaking = Cardio
- Writing = Stretching

And you can use the Think, Speak, Write Mindset Workout Method to work out your Optimism Muscles.

Think back to your school days. You routinely used thinking, speaking, and writing as tools to train your brain to remember information and learn new patterns. You might not have realized it, but that was your first mental gym! Just because you're not in school anymore doesn't mean you can't get a good mental workout. In this chapter, I'll show you how to think, speak, and write yourself to more joy, happiness, and peace.

Thinking: Strength Training for Your Mind

One of the main ways teachers help us learn is by asking questions. Questions are powerful emotional tools because they direct your focus. Asking a negative question like "What went wrong?" will direct your focus and attention toward a negative. But asking a positive question like "What went well?" will direct your focus and attention toward a positive. When you only ask and answer negative questions, you over-strengthen your pessimism muscles. To perform "strength training" for your Optimism Muscles, simply think about the answer to a positive question.

Anytime you mentally think about the answer to a positive question, you train your brain for positivity. For example, try spending one to two minutes each day thinking about the answer to the question "What am I grateful for?" By doing so over time, you will strengthen your gratitude muscles and experience more joy and contentment.

There are other muscles you can strengthen too, with positive questions like these:

- What are my strengths?
- Who did I help today?
- What acts of kindness and love have I received?
- What do I appreciate about this person?
- How can I add fun to my days?

The more positive questions you ask, the more you'll train your mind to look for, notice, and experience positivity—which leads to greater feelings of joy and peace. To train your Optimism Muscles, use positive questions as your weights.

Speaking: Cardio for Your Mind

Pop quiz! Complete the song lyrics:

- "Amazing grace..."
- "O say can you see..."
- "Sweet Caroline..."

Ba, ba, ba...Did you just naturally start singing? This demonstrates the power of repetition in training your brain to follow a pattern. Just hearing the first two or three notes of a well-known song can instantly trigger the lyrics to come straight into our minds.

But why is this? Speaking uses different neural pathways than simply thinking. Repetitively saying and hearing something incorporates your auditory learning processes and enhances how fast you learn. Why else would we sing "The ABC Song" to toddlers over and over?

If the "songs" you've been singing are mostly negative ("My life sucks," "I'm a failure," "Nobody cares about me"), then your brain will reflexively go down that path and complete the negative lyrics anytime the music gets cued up.

I'm using songs as a metaphor for your self-talk, but I actually have a friend who said during a tough time, she noticed her music choices caused her to keep feeling depressed, because all she listened to were sad songs that negatively influenced her mindset. There's a time and a place for a sad song, and I admit that Mary J. Blige got me through multiple breakups. But be mindful about what your ears hear, especially from your own mouth.

Luckily, you can retrain your brain by repetitively "singing" more positive songs. Your voice is a powerful instrument of change, and what you say carries a lot of weight in your brain. If you want your brain to learn a thinking pattern even faster, use your voice to say it out loud. For example, to do cardio for your gratitude muscles, repeat these three affirmations three times each:

- "There are good things in my life."
- "I am grateful for all the good in my life."
- "I am truly blessed."

I refer to this sequence as a three-by-three cardio circuit!

In addition to repeating affirmations and talking out loud to yourself, you can also talk to other people. Positive conversations create positive emotions. To exercise your gratitude muscles, you could talk to someone about what you're grateful for or go around the dinner table and invite each person to say what they're grateful for. Regularly talking about positives strengthens your brain's connection to positives, and when you tell your brain that something is important by regularly talking about it, your brain will continually look for that thing.

So, to recap, you can do cardio for your Optimism Muscles by (1) repeating positive statements or affirmations out loud and (2) having a positive conversation or sharing positive thoughts with someone else.

Regular mental cardio can train your brain to follow a more positive pattern to joy, happiness, and peace. To condition your mind, hop on a mental treadmill and use your voice to walk through phrases that represent your emotional goals.

Writing: Stretching for Your Mind

Obviously, anything you can think and say you can also write. Writing uses yet another set of neural pathways, and by incorporating visual and kinesthetic processes, writing can further enhance learning. Because writing is so effective at training your mind, I recommend experimenting with journaling.

Journaling could be used as a base to train all of your core Optimism Muscles. You could focus on one individual muscle at a time and spend weeks journaling one to three things daily that you're grateful for, then move to journaling one to three things daily that you did well or appreciate about yourself, and then finally focus on journaling one to three things daily that you appreciate about other people. This is how I set up the Optimism Challenge for you in Part 4.

However, sometimes in my personal journal, I write to work out all three core Optimism Muscles on the same day, with entries like these: "I am grateful it was a sunny day. I was so creative when I gave my presentation. I really appreciate my mom's sense of fashion."

There's no one perfect or best way to journal, so it's okay to be creative and try different things. But if you're a beginner, I suggest keeping it simple and writing one to three good things related to the Optimism Muscle you're trying to strengthen.

Another bonus to writing is that it creates a record of positivity that you can go back to and review weeks or months later if you hit a rough patch or need positive reminders. Writing positive thoughts down on paper stretches your Optimism Muscles, and when your mind is more flexible, you can reach deeper into positive places. As you write, tap into what is heartfelt and let your instincts be your guide.

The Mindset Workout Method

Now that you understand the importance of thinking, speaking, and writing for working out your Optimism Muscles, I'm going to show you how to bring all these elements together using my Think, Speak, Write Mindset Workout Method.

A Mindset Workout is set up like a traditional physical workout, including a warm-up, strength training, cardio, and then stretching for your mind. This method works well because it incorporates multiple forms of learning, but I also want you to feel empowered to use your wisdom and creativity to come up with a routine that works best for you. Let's break it down.

Breathe to Warm Up

Warming up with deep breathing helps to put your brain in a state of mindfulness, and when you're more grounded in the present moment, your cognitive abilities are heightened, allowing you to learn faster.

Think to Strengthen

Once your brain is ready to learn, strengthen a new or existing pattern by thinking about the answer to a positive question. Visualize and see the positive in your mind's eye to deepen the training effect.

Speak for Cardio

After strength training, do some cardio. Use your voice to help record the positive thoughts into your subconscious mind by repeating positive affirmations connected to your emotional goal.

Write to Stretch

After you've done some mental strength training and cardio, finish off with some mental stretching by writing in your journal.

The Mindset Workout Method is simple. Just think, speak, and write.

Five Minutes a Day to Joy and Peace

The first step in creating a Mindset Workout is to determine your emotional goal. Then, it's just a matter of doing exercises to build up the mental muscles that generate your goal emotions. If you want to feel more joy, happiness, and contentment, you might create a mental workout routine around gratitude. Below is a sample workout that incorporates a warm-up, strength training, cardio, and stretching for your gratitude muscles.

COACHING ACTION:
DAILY FIVE-MINUTE GRATITUDE WORKOUT

1. **Warm-Up:** Take three to five deep breaths to prepare your mind and ground you in the present moment.

2. **Strength Training:** Spend one to two minutes thinking about the answer to the positive question "What am I grateful for?"

3. **Cardio:** Repeat the affirmations "There are good things in my life," "I am grateful for all the good in my life," and "I am truly blessed," three to five times.

4. **Stretching:** Write down one to three things that you're grateful for in your journal.

When it comes to working out your Optimism Muscles, you can devote as much time as you'd like, but you don't have to spend hours a day to get results. You can train your brain for positivity in as little as five minutes a day, and I've seen short daily Mindset Workouts like the one above have a dramatic effect on my clients' emotional well-being.

For an even shorter mental workout (one to two minutes), just do any one part. Take a few deep breaths, or think about the answer to one positive question, or repeat a positive affirmation, or make a quick, positive journal entry.

Many people enjoy a daily routine because it helps keep the consistency flowing, but you may find that devoting five to ten minutes three times a week is enough mental working out to start creating more joy, happiness, and peace of mind.

Thinking, speaking, and writing are the core of the Mindset Workout, so I recommend focusing most of your time on these elements. But if you want to go a step further, you can incorporate body and behavior to enhance the mental training effect.

Act: Using Body and Behavior to Reinforce Mind

Since emotions are also influenced by body and behavior, once you think, speak, and write to train your mindset, you can reinforce positive changes with your actions.

Body

Physically embodying the desired mental shift can enhance the positivity you feel from your mind. Your heart rate and posture influence your emotional state. If you're trying to cultivate a higher-energy positive emotion like confidence, you might do something to slightly elevate your heart rate and adopt a posture that you associate with confidence while you work out your mind. If you're trying to cultivate a lower-energy positive emotion like serenity, you might slow down your heart rate and adopt a posture that makes you feel grounded.

Behavior

Once you activate a positive mindset, you can use behavior to further ingrain the shift in your thinking. Let your mindset guide your actions, and let your actions reinforce your mindset. For example, you can deepen feelings of gratitude by outwardly expressing your gratitude in both words and deeds, and you can show love and appreciation to yourself by engaging in self-care activities. To make a mindset shift, you must focus on training your mind, but your body and behavior can enhance your learning.

Exercise Is Magical

I'm guessing you've already experienced the magic of physical exercise. When you're physically strong, you can climb stairs with ten grocery bags because you only want to make one trip, and you can pick up stuff off the floor without having to call the chiropractor. Well, with strong Optimism Muscles, you'll be better at holding back fears, carrying life's inevitable disappointments, and running after your dreams. Strong quads, glutes, and core muscles help you win races. Strong gratitude, appreciation, and confidence help you win life.

Mind Care and Mindset Workouts are key to mental and emotional health. And you can think, speak, and write your way to more joy, happiness, and peace. Use breathing as your warm-up, positive questions as your weights, affirmations and conversations as your cardio, and written words as your stretches.

The following chapters are devoted to taking a deeper dive into each of your Optimism Muscles, so you'll know which ones to work out for your emotional goals.

 UP YOUR OPTIMISM GAME: COACH'S CORNER 😊

I know you're busy. That's why I designed the Think, Speak, Write Mindset Workout Method to be short and effective. If you want more joy and peace, start with a daily five-minute optimism workout. You can do it first thing in the morning, at lunch, before bed, or at any other time you want a mental reset. Five short minutes will make a huge difference in your day.

Also, working out your mind should be fun and engaging. So, you don't have to force yourself to do everything if it doesn't resonate. I've seen people get physically healthy just doing yoga, or running, or weight training.

If you love writing, it's okay to focus mostly on journaling. If you love talking, it's okay to focus on affirmations and conversation. And if you like doing deep thought work on your own, then by all means, lean into pondering positive questions. As long as you're exercising your mind, your optimism will get stronger—and you'll reap the emotional rewards.

SEVEN

GRATITUDE MUSCLES

"Gratitude unlocks the fullness of life. It turns what we have into enough, and more. It turns denial into acceptance, chaos to order, confusion to clarity."
—MELODY BEATTIE

AT A YOUNG AGE, I REMEMBER MY GREAT-GRAND-mother Maw Maw telling me to count my blessings, but I shrugged it off as something that old people say, like "Eat your spinach, so you can be strong like Popeye" or "Put on a hat, so you don't catch a cold." Being raised by a single mom, my sister and I didn't have a lot of material things, but overall, I was a pretty happy kid.

Then, when I got to high school and started seeing other kids with polo shirts, Girbaud jeans, Air Jordans, and gold jewelry, I started to feel a lot less satisfied with my life. For a while, I chased money and success, trying to fill what I perceived as a void. Now that I'm older, I can truly see the wisdom in Maw

Maw's words, and I'm guessing there's been someone in your life who has also advised you to count your blessings.

When your gratitude muscles are weak, you're more likely to feel depressed, anxious, and frustrated. You may feel sad initially that you don't have something and then anxious that you'll never be successful. Finally, frustration can set in as you constantly chase what eludes you. But here's the weird thing about accomplishment: You can achieve all the success in the world and still feel depressed, unfulfilled, and dissatisfied, if you lose your ability to be grateful. Regardless of your circumstances, strong gratitude muscles will help you walk through life with more joy, happiness, and contentment.

Gratitude Journaling: Writing to Build Joy, Happiness, and Contentment

In one study, researchers invited depressed participants to practice a simple behavior shift. Each day for one week, the participants were asked to write down three good things or three daily blessings in a journal and reflect on the causes. At the end of the week, the participants showed a decrease in depression and an increase in happiness. Even cooler, when researchers followed up with the participants months later, they still showed an increase in happiness, even though many had stopped formally practicing gratitude.*

---

* M.E.P. Seligman et al., "Positive Psychology Progress: Empirical Validation of Interventions," *American Psychologist* 60, no. 5 (2005): 410–21, https://doi. org/10.1037/0003-066X.60.5.410.

Many other studies have also found that practicing gratitude can decrease stress, depression, and anxiety. That's why gratitude is one of the core Optimism Muscles. Just like the participants in the study above, you can also train your mind to be more grateful by developing the habit of looking for the good in life. And once you've adopted a more positive mindset, you can continually reap the emotional benefits.

If you're new to gratitude journaling, you may wonder what to write. Really, there aren't many rules, just a whole bunch of things you *can* try if the mood suits you.

First, with regard to time, you can write about something that happened today, recently, or further back in the past. And you can be as specific as you'd like. You can write a general entry like "I'm grateful for my friends," or you can make it more personal by adding names and why you're grateful for them (e.g., "I'm grateful that Tom picked up my son from practice").

You can also be grateful for your body, senses, and physical abilities. Maybe you take sight, hearing, smell, taste, and touch for granted, but your senses allow you to experience everything good in your life. You can see beautiful landscapes, smell apple pie, taste chocolate, hear music, and hug loved ones. If you're blessed to have working legs, your body allows you the independence to move freely in the world. Not everyone can see, hear, or walk without assistance.

You can also be grateful for small things like a cup of coffee, a smile on someone's face, a pair of shoes, or your favorite dish at a restaurant. You can be grateful for nature—the sun, the earth, the ocean, the birds, the bees, the flowers, and the trees. All that is life-giving comes from nature.

Finally, you can be grateful for your comforts, conveniences, and technology. My grandfather was born in 1924 and thought the radio was one of the most amazing technological advances. Now we have cell phones, microwaves, computers, the internet, delivery services for everything imaginable, and many modern conveniences previous generations didn't have.

This list is far from exhaustive—just a few suggestions to help you get your creativity flowing. Once you start looking, you'll find there is so much you can choose to be grateful for. When you train your brain to notice all the good things around you, you'll feel more joy and contentment.

Major Exercise: Gratitude Letter

In the six-week Optimism Challenge I outline in Part 4, I'll suggest that you choose at least one major exercise to complete. The three options are: Gratitude Letter, Strengths Résumé, and Beautiful Day. I'll explain the latter two in upcoming chapters, but here, we'll start with the Gratitude Letter.

When Ashley came to see me, she had a history of depression and wanted to develop more joy, so I recommended a four-week program to up her gratitude game. One of the exercises in the program was to write a Gratitude Letter, but we had no idea the impact this exercise would have.

Ashley had a strained relationship with her elderly mother. At one point, they went more than three years without speaking to each other. They'd been trying to reconcile but never felt truly connected. Ashley realized that she always harped on what her mom didn't do for her, so she decided to try gratitude. She spent weeks thinking back on all the things she appreciated about her mom and ended up with a six-page letter.

For Mother's Day, she flew to visit her mom and surprised her by reading the letter to her after dinner. They both cried, and when she finished, her mom responded, "I never knew you thought those things about me. Now I can die in peace." It was a peak moment in their relationship, and it brought them closer than they had ever been.

Parents often live with guilt and shame about what they could not do for their kids, but hearing deep gratitude from their adult children can be life-changing. A heartfelt Gratitude Letter can create so much joy! So, tell your parents, kids, partner, friends, and mentors why you are grateful for them.

For this exercise, simply pick someone you'd like to thank, and write them a letter of gratitude. Plan to spend some time and energy on this. If you want to share the letter with a loved one on a particular day like Ashely did, don't wait until the last minute to start.

Gratitude Letters are just one of the many ways you can strengthen your gratitude muscles. Writing these letters can boost your joy and strengthen your relationships—even if you never share them or you write to someone who has passed away. If shared, both parties benefit, so consider sending your letter by mail or reading it aloud during a visit. You don't have to write six pages like Ashley did. Just write from the heart, and aim for at least two hundred to three hundred words.

Exercises and Emotions

In each muscle chapter, I'll give you mindset and behavioral exercise ideas for that muscle. Mindset exercises will revolve around strength training, cardio, and stretching for your mind using the Think, Speak, Write Mindset Workout Method, and behavioral exercises will be actions you can do to create and reinforce positive emotions.

I'll also include a quick emotion guide that lists some of the positive emotions you'll feel when the muscles are strong and potential negative emotions you'll feel when they're weak. Your emotions are not limited to those listed, but you can use the summary boxes in each muscle chapter to determine which Optimism Muscles you want to work out.

GRATITUDE MUSCLES: QUICK EMOTION GUIDE

- **Strong**: joy, happiness, contentment, peace
- **Weak**: depression, anxiety, frustration, discontent, anger, jealousy

---

Think, Speak, Write Mindset Workout Ideas

Strength Training: Positive Question to Think About

- *What am I grateful for?*

Cardio: Positive Affirmations

- *There are good things in my life.*
- *I am grateful for all the good in my life.*
- *I am truly blessed.*

Cardio: Conversation

Talk with someone about what you're grateful for. Ask others about what they are grateful for.

Stretching: Journal Prompt

- *What am I grateful for?*

Additional Exercises

Three Good Things

Write one to three things that you're grateful for over one to six weeks.

Gratitude Before Meals

Say grace or pause for a moment of gratitude before meals.

Gratitude Roundtable

When gathering with friends, family, or a team of people, take turns going around the room and sharing one thing you're each grateful for.

UP YOUR OPTIMISM GAME: COACH'S CORNER 

A little gratitude can go a long way toward boosting your joy and peace. But gratitude doesn't mean giving up on your hopes and dreams. In fact, vision and dreaming are also Optimism Muscles, because pursuing meaningful goals and accomplishing worthy achievements generates many positive emotions. So, you can still strive for better health, more money, or deeper connection, but along the way, practice looking for the good in life. That way, you'll have a more joyful journey.

EIGHT

SELF-APPRECIATION MUSCLES

*"Too many people overvalue what they
are not and undervalue what they are."*
—MALCOLM S. FORBES

EVER SINCE CHILDHOOD, KRISTEN HAD HATED MAKing mistakes.

"One time in fifth grade, I actually cried after getting an A on a test," she told me.

"Why?" I asked.

"Because," she said, "I got one answer wrong."

In high school, she became critical of her appearance and athletic ability. In college, she was self-critical about her lack of money and life experience. When she started working, she compared herself negatively to her colleagues, and when she became a mother for the first time, she felt inadequate because of all the things she couldn't do or failed to do perfectly for her daughter.

Kristen's strong self-criticism muscles created a cycle of anxiety and depression. She was anxious because she was afraid of making mistakes and wanted to do everything perfectly—and when the inevitable mistake occurred, she'd beat herself up and feel depressed.

Clearly, Kristen was already really good at finding her flaws. I wanted to help her get better at finding her strengths.

It's common to be our own worst critics, and habitual and harsh self-criticism is a source of many negative emotions. When you continually focus on your flaws, weaknesses, and mistakes, you're likely to feel anxious, depressed, inadequate, overwhelmed, and even mad at yourself.

But the opposite of self-criticism is self-appreciation, your second core Optimism Muscle. Self-appreciation develops when you focus on your strengths, abilities, good deeds, successes, and contributions. When you strengthen your ability to look for and see the good in yourself, you'll feel joyful, proud, confident, grounded, self-assured, motivated, and at peace.

Strengths: The Language of Self-Appreciation

I often recommend that my clients take the Values in Action (VIA) Character Strengths Survey developed by positive psychology pioneers Martin Seligman and Christopher Peterson. According to the VIA, the twenty-four universal character strengths are creativity, curiosity, judgment, love of learning, perspective, bravery, perseverance, honesty, zest, love, kindness, social intelligence, teamwork, fairness, leadership, forgiveness, humility, prudence, self-regulation, appreciation of beauty and excellence, gratitude, hope, humor, and spirituality.

You have all these strengths inside you, but some characteristics will be your top strengths. When Kristen took the VIA assessment, her top five strengths were kindness, curiosity, love of learning, prudence, and perseverance. This knowledge gave her the language to describe her strengths and notice them in action. With this new perspective on her strengths, I asked her to tell me about a time when she displayed perseverance.

"When my daughters were five and nine, I decided to go back to school to get a master's degree," she told me. "I was working full-time, so it was intense. Once I put them to bed, I was up all night, reading and doing assignments. There were many times I told my husband I was thinking about quitting. But I wanted to advance in my career and teach my daughters the value of education and hard work, so I just kept pushing. And earning my master's degree is one of my proudest accomplishments."

As Kristen told me the story, she sat up a little taller, and I could hear the confidence in her voice. Once she became aware of how focusing on her strengths, successes, and contributions directly resulted in her feeling more joy, confidence, and pride, she decided to use her love of learning and perseverance to continue strengthening her self-appreciation muscles.

I may not know you personally, but I know you have talents and gifts that make you unique and wonderful. And I'm willing to bet that you've accomplished great things in your life and have made positive contributions to your company, community, and family. Appreciation is the antidote to criticism. Learning how to appreciate yourself will transform your self-talk, turn down the volume of your inner critic, and dramatically change your relationship with yourself. Also, when you love and appreciate yourself, it will shape the example you set for others and lead you to more joy, happiness, and inner peace.

COACHING ACTION: KNOW YOUR STRENGTHS

Take the free VIA Character Strengths Survey at *viacharacter.org* to identify your top five strengths.

Self-Appreciation Journaling:
Writing to Build Confidence and Self-Love

As with gratitude, you can write about your strengths and accomplishments to work out your self-appreciation muscles. You can think about what you appreciate about yourself in general, including your abilities, personality, and characteristics. For example, I appreciate my kindness, sense of humor, intellect, singing voice, running ability, cooking skills, sense of fashion, determination, leadership, boldness, and creativity.

Or you can think about the good you do in specific arenas, such as at home, at work, or in the community. What strengths, skills, or experience do you bring to each arena, and how are those abilities helping you make a positive contribution?

Lastly, you can think about the good you do in relationships—as a mother, father, son, daughter, brother, sister, spouse, partner, friend, colleague, or citizen of the world. Who are you helping, uplifting, and supporting through your words, deeds, and presence? When have you been kind, compassionate, patient, or forgiving? How have you made someone's day, even if it was just a small gesture like sending a text, holding open a door, or flashing your smile?

Not Good Enough

I know self-appreciation can feel awkward and even wrong in the beginning, because growing up, many of us were taught that pride is bad. But if you label feeling proud as bad, you will try to avoid it—and you'll feel guilty if you experience it, which will reinforce your attempts to avoid it. This is a common thinking trap that leads to feelings of inadequacy, shame, anxiety, and depression.

You do a good job, but you don't want to say that you did a good job. As a result, you feel inadequate, unsatisfied, and not good enough, which leads to an endless cycle of criticism and perfectionism. You're internalizing a belief like this: *I don't think I'm good, so I have to keep working endlessly until I get good enough. But because I never allow myself to feel proud, I'm never good enough.*

There's nothing wrong with having high standards and a desire to produce quality work, but if you're overly critical, you may never feel satisfied with yourself or your contributions. Self-appreciation can help to break the cycle of criticism and perfectionism, allowing you to feel more positive about yourself and the work that you do.

Impostor Syndrome

Do you have multiple college degrees, years of work experience, and a long list of challenges that you've overcome to achieve academic, athletic, or career success, yet when someone asks you to lead a meeting, give a presentation, or write an article, you freak out? No judgment.

There's a sneaky perfectionistic thinking trap that educated people often get caught in. When you know something for sure, you're really confident, but when you study any subject deeply, you realize just how much you still don't know about the topic. In order to feel confident, you believe you have to know for sure: *If I just learn more, then I'll feel confident.*

But knowledge is infinite, and since you can always learn more, you can get stuck in an endless cycle of anxiety, inadequacy, and pressure to learn more. And the crazy thing is sometimes the more you learn, the less confident you become, because you get hyperfocused on what you don't know and completely ignore what you *do* know.

Being hypercritical leads to less confidence. Harping on your flaws and downplaying your knowledge, skills, and abilities can make any task feel too big. *I don't have this credential. I'm not experienced. I didn't go to Harvard.* When you focus on what you are *not*, you'll feel like an impostor. But when you focus on the good that you *are*, you'll be up for any challenge.

In order to shine brightly and play a bigger game, you've got to embrace all your goodness. What are your superpowers? What have you already accomplished? What skills do you have? Sure, there's always more to learn and do. But you already know a lot, and you've already done a lot. So, take a moment to appreciate all that you already are!

Major Exercise: Strengths Résumé

One day, while updating my LinkedIn profile and reviewing all my certifications, degrees, and experiences, I felt a sense of pride and confidence about my career. That's when I created the Strengths Résumé exercise. The idea is to build a list of your peak moments and strengths in action to show yourself that you are a worthy and capable person.

When were you brave, persistent, loving, or creative? Your entry on each moment can be fifty to one hundred words or several paragraphs long. Your regular résumé is designed to show value to an employer. When you update your Strengths Résumé, you show your value to *yourself.*

Writing stories about your strengths gives you evidence of your ability and character, which supports you in feeling joyful, proud, and confident. Creating one entry for your Strengths Résumé is a major exercise in the six-week Optimism Challenge, and below are some additional ways to build your self-appreciation muscles.

SELF-APPRECIATION MUSCLES: QUICK EMOTION GUIDE

- **Strong**: joy, pride, confidence, grounding, self-assurance, motivation, peace with self
- **Weak**: inadequacy, anxiety, depression, shame, overwhelm, anger toward self

---

Think, Speak, Write Mindset Workout Ideas

Strength Training: Positive Questions to Think About

- *What are my strengths?*
- *What do I appreciate about myself?*
- *What positive contributions have I made?*

Cardio: Positive Affirmations

Affirming Strengths

- *I have strengths and abilities.*
- *I look for the good in myself.*
- *I am _______.* (Insert an adjective that describes your strength or quality, such as *kind, wise, persistent, creative,* or *funny*.)

Cardio: Conversation

Talk about your strengths, successes, and good deeds. Ask others what they think you're good at.

Stretching: Journal Prompts

- *What are my strengths?*
- *What did I do well?*

Additional Exercises

Three Good Things About Me

Each day, write one to three good things about yourself. You can use the strengths from the VIA Character Strengths Survey as prompts, focusing slightly more on your top five. For example, if one of your top strengths is kindness, you can ask questions like these:

- *Who did I lift up today?*
- *What strengths did I display today?*
- *How did I make a positive impact?*

Here are sample entries:

- I was patient and kind when my son made a mistake.
- I showed determination to finish the project.
- I took care of myself by doing yoga.

Peak Moment Story

Tell someone about a peak moment in your life when you used inner strengths to do something you're proud of. Add this story to your Strengths Résumé.

UP YOUR OPTIMISM GAME: COACH'S CORNER 

To tame your inner critic, practice looking for the good in yourself. Thinking, speaking, and writing about your best moments will provide evidence of your abilities and help you relate to yourself in a more positive and appreciative way.

You might have to start out with one-pound self-appreciation weights, but I know you can grow into a confident, self-assured, and proud person. There is so much evidence of your goodness; you just have to get better at noticing, appreciating, and embracing it.

NINE

APPRECIATION OF OTHERS MUSCLES

*"The roots of all goodness lie in the
soil of appreciation for goodness."*
—DALAI LAMA

AS A LEADER, JOE WAS IMPATIENT AND HAD A SHORT fuse. He constantly looked for mistakes and criticized flaws. The lawyer in him liked debating, and he was quick to dissect and debunk every idea, coming up with reasons why it wouldn't work. But after a stretch of negative exit interviews, Joe started to rethink how he wanted to lead.

Earlier, I asked you to experiment by thinking about a time someone close to you hurt you. Then, I asked you to think about a time the same person had your back, to see what emotions might come up.

I took a similar approach with Joe. Kicking off our session, I asked, "Can you tell me about a time someone close to you let you down?"

"What pops into my mind is the time my ex-wife, Carol, ruined Thanksgiving," Joe said. "It was early in our marriage, and it was the first time we hosted my mom and dad for the holiday. I wanted everything to go perfectly, but Carol messed up the turkey, accidentally bought a pumpkin pie instead of sweet potato, and dropped the casserole on the floor. We argued the whole day. It was the worst."

"How do you feel focusing on this time?" I asked.

"Mad, frustrated, and disappointed," he said. "It gets my blood boiling every time I think about it."

Then I asked him to tell me about a time Carol really came through for him. After a long pause, Joe replied, "When I had knee surgery, she really took care of me. My knee got infected, and it was so swollen and painful that I could barely walk. I was not the best patient, but she was understanding and caring. She did all the shopping, cooking, and cleaning—and nursed me back to health."

"How do you feel focusing on this time?" I asked.

"I feel lucky, blessed, and grateful."

The experience was eye-opening for Joe. He often blamed his anger on the "stupidity," weaknesses, and flaws of others. However, when he realized he was making *himself* angry by looking at everyone through a critical lens, he committed to becoming more appreciative of others.

Do It for Yourself

People aren't perfect. Parents, partners, and kids are not perfect. If you develop the habit of viewing everyone around you through a negative lens, always focusing on their flaws, weaknesses, and mistakes, you're more likely to feel anger, frustration, anxiety, depression, and tension in your relationships.

By contrast, looking for the good in others helps you feel more positive emotions. If you develop an appreciative eye for other people's strengths, abilities, good deeds, and contributions, you're more likely to feel empathy, trust, love, pride, and gratitude. Appreciation of others can transform your emotions, increase your sense of connection, and strengthen your relationships. Much of your happiness and peace of mind come from the quality of your relationships, which is why appreciation of others is your third core Optimism Muscle.

Transforming Relationships

Many people think of connection as something you do physically, but it's also a mental skill. Negativity and criticism repel; positivity and appreciation attract. Focusing on someone's flaws will repel you away from them, but focusing on their goodness will draw you toward them. In addition, when you express your negativity to someone, they will be repelled away from you, but when you express your appreciation, they will be drawn toward you. Negativity—in thoughts, words, or actions—weakens connection. Positivity strengthens it.

I've seen relationships dramatically change when one person decided to get better at looking for and expressing the good in the other person. I know: Relationships are complicated. Still, you can repair, rekindle, and strengthen them by building stronger appreciation of others muscles.

Appreciation of Others Journaling:
Writing to Build Love and Connection

To supercharge your sense of love, gratitude, and connection, you can journal about the good you see in others at home, in your close relationships, at work, in the community, and in the world. If there is a specific relationship you want to strengthen, you can point your appreciation in that direction. For example, if you want to feel closer to your partner, start journaling one to three things that you appreciate about them. Over time, this exercise can decrease anger and frustration, while increasing love, connection, and gratitude in that relationship.

You can also practice appreciation of others in general and look for the good in your friends, family, and colleagues. When you journal, think back on your day and write one to three things that you appreciate about other people. You can even appreciate people through technology and journal good things you witnessed on TV or the internet, from extraordinary feats by athletes, performers, and great leaders to regular citizens doing good work in the community.

You can use the language of strengths from the VIA (see last chapter) to build your appreciation of others muscles. Look for times when people are kind, funny, and creative. Look for excellence, perseverance, and bravery. The better you get at spotting and appreciating the good in others, the more positive emotions you'll feel toward them and the stronger your connections and relationships will become.

Optimistic Leadership

When I was twelve, my cousin and I tried out for our town's baseball team. The most skilled kids ended up on the A team, and the next best players on the B team. Being brand new to baseball, my cousin and I ended up on the same C team, and I kid you not: We were the real-life Bad News Bears. We couldn't throw, catch, or hit the ball to save our lives. But we had a secret weapon: Coach Gary!

Coach Gary was an encourager who kept looking for our strengths. He initially put me in left field because I was fast and had a strong arm. Even if I didn't catch the ball, I could get it back into the infield. My cousin was fast and had the best glove, so Coach put him in center field. We all made mistake after mistake, but Coach kept cheering us on and focusing on the good that he saw, especially our effort.

After a few games, he pulled me aside and said, "I think you would be a great catcher, because you have a strong arm. I'll teach you if you're willing to give it a shot." I agreed.

This was coaching at its best. He looked for our strengths and tried to put us in the best position to shine, and we didn't let him down. As a catcher, I started throwing out so many runners that people stopped attempting to steal bases, and our team went on to win the C league championship. We all loved Coach Gary, and his optimistic leadership style helped us grow and play at our best.

My client Joe's high school football coach was much different. He was a tough, hard-charging, "my way or the highway" kinda guy, and because Joe grew so much under his coach's tough-love approach, he adopted a more authoritarian leadership style himself—with the negative consequences I described at the beginning of this chapter.

When you communicate negativity and harsh criticism as a leader, parent, teacher, or coach, it's more likely that the person you're leading will feel emotions like anger, frustration, overwhelm, anxiety, or depression. There is a time and a place for constructive feedback, but be mindful that if you lead from an overly pessimistic mindset, the people you lead will feel more negative emotions. By looking for and expressing the good you see as a leader, you can inspire people to be the best versions of themselves.

Your current relationship and leadership styles may be more critical than appreciative, but you can evolve. As you develop the skill of appreciating the good in others, you will increase the positive emotions that both sides experience and increase the strength of your connections.

APPRECIATION OF OTHERS MUSCLES: QUICK EMOTION GUIDE

- **Strong**: empathy, connection, love, trust, pride, gratitude
- **Weak**: anger, frustration, contempt, anxiety, depression

Think, Speak, Write Mindset Workout Ideas

Strength Training: Positive Questions to Think About

- *What do I appreciate about _________? (Insert person's name.)*
- *What strengths and good deeds did I notice in someone else?*
- *What did _________ do well? (Insert person's name.)*

Cardio: Positive Affirmations

- *I look for the good in others.*
- *Everyone has strengths and abilities.*
- *I appreciate the good that I see.*

Cardio: Conversation

Tell someone what you appreciate about them or other people.

Stretching: Journal Prompts

- *What do I appreciate about others?* (Use a specific name to strengthen that connection.)
- *What good did I see others display?*

Additional Exercises

Three Good Things About Others

Simply journal one to three good things that you appreciated about other people that day.

Strength Glasses

When you witness someone do something that you want to be critical of, try putting on your "strength glasses" to see which strengths they are using. For example, being nosy and asking a lot of questions could indicate the strengths of curiosity and love of learning. Being "overly emotional" could flow from the strengths of compassion and fairness. Being tough and all business could draw on the strengths of courage and leadership.

Most of the time, people are doing their best to be good citizens, and their unique strengths will determine how they walk through life. So, practice noticing and appreciating others' strengths.

I know people can be frustrating and annoying, but they can also be brilliant and amazing. Remember, connection begins in the mind. When you focus on the good, you'll feel more love, connection, and gratitude, and when you express your appreciation, the other person will feel the same good vibes.

Bringing the Three Core Optimism Muscles Together

If you spend all your time focusing on what you don't have, what's wrong with the world, your past failures, what you don't like about yourself, what you hate about your body, other people's mistakes, and other people's flaws, you're going to feel stressed, depressed, and anxious.

But optimism is a skill that you can learn and improve. With a little bit of practice, you can find your positivity groove. You can up your gratitude game and get your self-appreciation on point. Start to see your strengths as your superpowers, and they'll propel you to what you want. And as you look for the best in others and see the good inside, in the end, you'll be the one who feels more joy and pride.

Strong core muscles provide the foundation for joy and peace, but they're just the beginning. In the next part, you'll learn the full extent of your optimism anatomy.

PART 2 SUMMARY: MASTER THE METHOD

1. **The Four Keys to Effective Optimism**: When practicing optimism, the thoughts you attempt to internalize must be (1) heartfelt and believable, (2) personally chosen, (3) at the right time, and (4) in the right dose.

2. **The Think, Speak, Write Mindset Workout Method**: In Optimism Muscle exercise terms, thinking is strength training, speaking is cardio, and writing is stretching.

3. **Three Core Optimism Muscles**: Your three core Optimism Muscles are (1) gratitude, focusing on the good in life; (2) self-appreciation, focusing on the good in yourself; and (3) appreciation of others, focusing on the good in others.

4. **The First Two Major Exercises**: To build gratitude muscles, try writing a Gratitude Letter to someone in your life. To build self-appreciation muscles, try creating a Strengths Résumé.

THE MUSCLES

OPTIMISM MUSCLE ANATOMY

Back in the day, if you hired me as your personal trainer and said you only had time to do three exercises, I would have recommended squats, push-ups, and pull-ups, or a machine version of those exercises, because those core movement patterns work nearly every muscle in your body and can get you in good shape. But for certain types of growth, you might need different exercises.

Gratitude, self-appreciation, and appreciation of others are like those squats, push-ups, and pull-ups. They are the core thinking patterns that lead to an optimistic and positive mindset. But there are additional mental muscles and countless exercises you can do to strengthen your optimism.

While the six-week Optimism Challenge in Part 4 centers on your three core Optimism Muscles, it's useful to get the full picture of your mental muscle anatomy, so you'll know how to generate an even wider range of positive emotions.

The following chapters cover your twenty-one additional Optimism Muscles. I'll share a few common emotions that you feel when each muscle is strong or weak and give you some sample mindset exercises for each muscle. As you read each chapter, think about how the mental muscle shows up in your emotional life, and consider how strengthening it may benefit you.

Optimism Muscles

Gratitude, Self-Appreciation, Appreciation of Others, Vision, Mindfulness, Savoring, Celebration (and Appreciation), Joy, Humor (and Fun), Love, Self-Compassion, Confidence, Courage, Awe (and Wonder), Serenity (and Acceptance), Agency (and Empowerment), Empathy, Agreeableness, Forgiveness, Meaning-Making (and Purpose), Dreaming (and Imagination), Passion (and Interest), Faith (and Trust), Hope

Pessimism Muscles

Ungratefulness, Self-Criticism, Criticism of Others, Aimlessness, Unawareness, Minimizing, Complaining, Misery, Seriousness, Hate, Self-Cruelty, Insecurity, Fearfulness, "Meh," Unrest, Disempowerment, Narcissism, Disagreeableness, Grudge-Holding, Meaningless-Making, Catastrophizing/Nightmare, Disinterest, Doubt, Despair

OPTIMISM Muscles

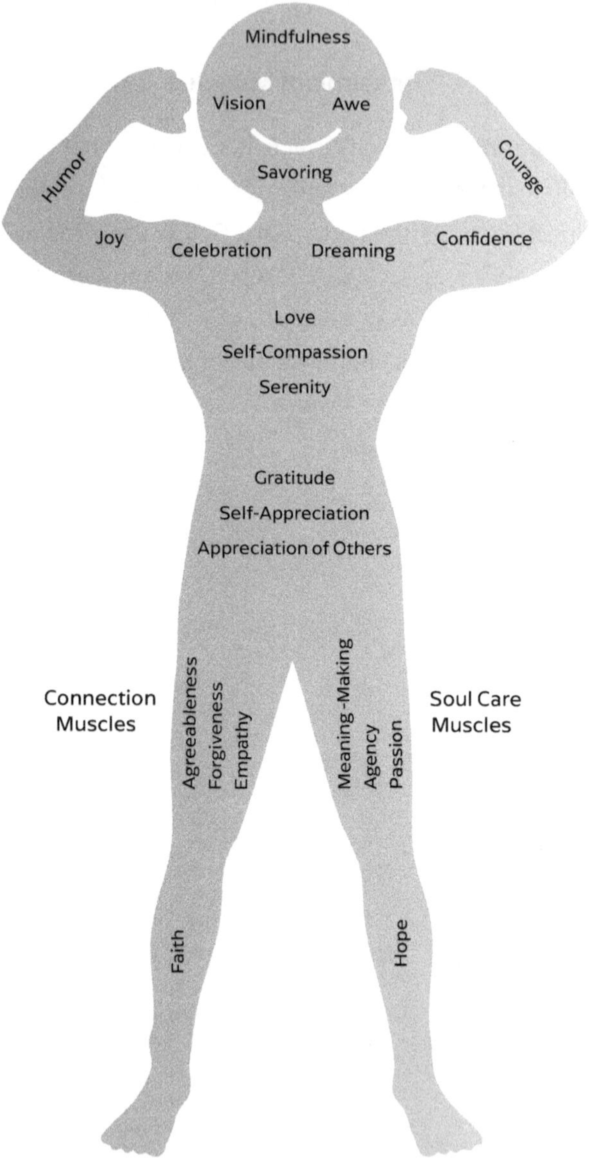

PESSIMISM Muscles

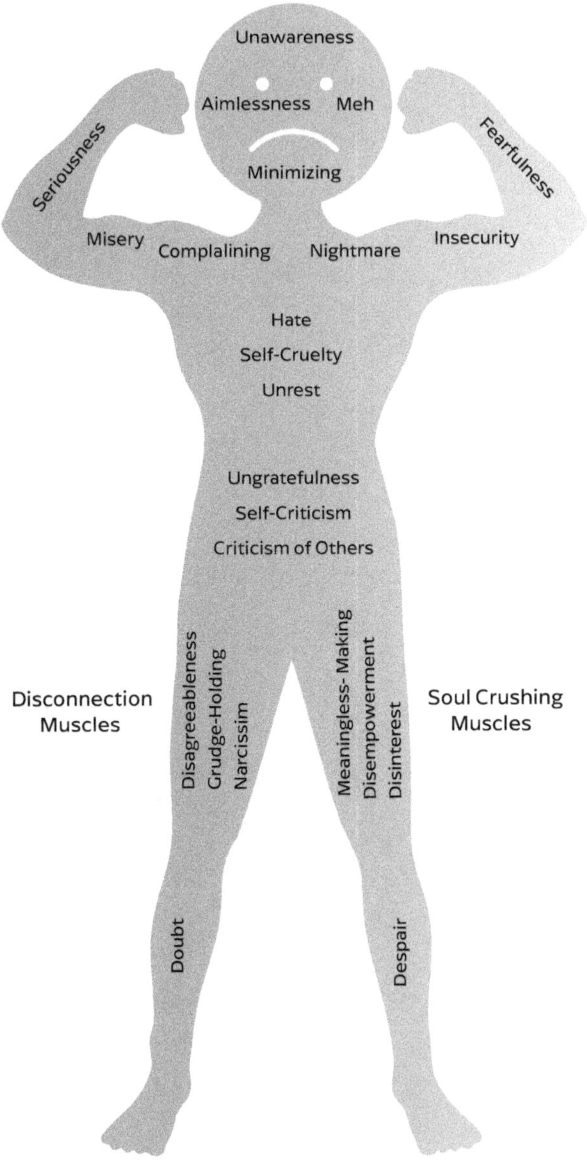

TEN

VISION MUSCLES

"Where there is no vision, the people perish."
—PROVERBS 29:18 (KJV)

WHEN I STARTED COACHING KRISTEN, ONE OF the first questions I asked her was "How do you want to be?" At first, it seemed like a weird question, because she was used to everyone asking her what she wanted to *do*. But you can do things in different ways. You can go to work miserably or joyfully. You can help out your family willingly or begrudgingly. You can walk through the world hatefully or lovingly.

One of the best ways to pump more positive emotions into your brain is to get better at focusing on what you want to be, have, or do. This is the essence of vision! Having a guiding star regarding what is important and meaningful can serve to make you feel more hopeful, excited, focused, and determined, and it can order your steps to create your life in a way that increases the chances you'll feel positive emotions.

When you don't have a clear vision, you're more likely to feel directionless, scattered, apathetic, depressed, or frustrated, and you might drift around emotionally like a rudderless boat. But setting emotional, life, and behavioral goals can help steer you in a positive direction.

Emotional Goals: Be

Your emotional well-being will suffer if you never take the time to identify your emotional goals. When setting goals, it's more powerful to focus on how you want to *be* rather than what you want to *avoid*. So, if you don't want to feel anxious, depressed, or angry, you might say that your emotional goals are to feel calm, grounded, joyful, happy, content, empathetic, or forgiving. Once you've identified the emotions that you want to feel more often, it's just a matter of strengthening the Optimism Muscles that generate your goal emotions.

COACHING QUESTION: YOUR EMOTIONAL TOP FIVE

What are the top three to five positive emotions that you want to feel more often?

Life Goals: Have

A key element of vision is identifying what's most important to you. Having worthy goals to pursue can ignite your spark.

You'll feel your best emotionally when you're living in alignment with your deepest values and most important goals, and you'll feel worse emotionally when you stray from the path that leads to your goals.

It took me around four years to write this book. The vision of being a best-selling author and sought-after speaker fueled my determination to keep going. Because it was such an important goal, I got frustrated when other responsibilities took me away from writing. But when I finally finished, nothing could stop the joy and pride from bursting out of me!

Achieving goals and making meaningful contributions add to your life satisfaction. But you have to tell your brain where you want it to take you. Without clear goals, you can easily spend a lot of time chasing shiny objects and focusing on things that are not that important. So, when you get better at identifying what's most important to you and spend more time focused on it, you'll feel more positive emotions.

What would you like to say is true about yourself six to twelve months from now?

Behavioral Goals: Do

Behavior is what brings your vision into reality. You can set SMART goals or intention goals to help guide your actions. A SMART goal is **s**pecific, **m**easurable, **a**ction-oriented, relevant, and time-bound, whereas an intention goal is a general instruction for your brain about how you want to live your life. For example, "Go to the gym three times a week" is a SMART goal, and "Move my body regularly" is an intention goal.

There are pros and cons to both. SMART goals sometimes feel restrictive and inflexible, but their specificity can make it easier to focus, because you know exactly what you're going to do. Intention goals are more flexible, but sometimes the lack of structure may make it harder to execute a plan. Kristen set an intention to be more joyful, and Joe set an intention to be more patient. Then, they used a daily SMART goal to practice. Use your wisdom as you experiment with both to see how they help you grow.

Creating Your Vision

A positive future vision is a narrative about how you want to live and what you want to do. It will pull you forward and give you hope, purpose, and direction. Here's a snippet of Kristen's vision:

> I am a loving mother, daughter, and wife who is close with my family. We laugh, play, and enjoy life together, and we are there for each other in tough times. I have the confidence to pursue my goals at work and in my personal life, and I regularly do mindset exercises to feel grounded, calm, and joyful. I am a positive role model for my daughters, and at the end of the day, I feel proud of my contribution and love myself deeply.

If you'd like, you can write a short Well-Being Vision Statement, so you'll have your own guiding star. But for now, here are some vision muscle workout ideas.

VISION MUSCLES: QUICK EMOTION GUIDE

- **Strong**: hope, excitement, joy, focus, determination
- **Weak**: aimlessness, feeling scattered, frustration, depression, apathy

---

Think, Speak, Write Mindset Workout Ideas

Strength Training: Positive Questions to Think About

- *What are my top values and priorities?*
- *What is really important to me?*
- *What do I want to be, have, or do?*

Cardio: Positive Affirmations

- *________ is important to me.* (Fill in the blank with *love, growth, honesty,* or whatever applies.)
- *I live in line with my values.*
- *I pursue my goals with passion.*

Cardio: Conversation

Talk to other people about your goals and what you want to accomplish.

Stretching: Journal Prompts

- *What would I like to accomplish?*
- *What goals would I like to pursue?*

Additional Exercises

Set Priorities

Write out a list of the top ten to twenty-five things that are most important to you. If you start to feel negative emotions, check to see if what you're focusing on is on your list. Use your list of what's important to guide your focus and behavior.

Envision the Coming Year

Create a six- to twelve-month well-being vision for yourself:

- Include your top three to five emotional goals.
- Specify SMART or intention behavioral goals to help you move toward your vision.
- Create a vision board.

 UP YOUR OPTIMISM GAME: COACH'S CORNER 

Having worthy goals helps you to generate meaning and purpose. But if you've failed to meet your goals in the past, you may be hesitant to set new ones, because you want to avoid negative emotions like disappointment and frustration. This is your negativity bias trying to protect you. However, there can be joy in the journey, no matter where you end up. If you reframe your goal as an experiment, you'll either succeed or learn from it.

Remember this question from the anatomy of motivation: *What if it works?*

The more time you spend focusing on your goals, the person you want to become, and things you want to do, the more success and joy you'll experience. So, flex your vision muscles, and go after your goals to put your mind on a positive path.

ELEVEN

MINDFULNESS MUSCLES

"Awareness is the greatest agent for change."
—ECKHART TOLLE

MINDFULNESS IS A STATE OF BEING AWARE OR conscious, and it's a master thinking skill. Developing awareness of what's happening in your body, life, and mind improves your ability to manage your emotions. Also, being mindful of your values and goals helps you to become more intentional about your choices.

The opposite of mindfulness is mindlessness. When your mindfulness muscles are weak, you are more likely to feel distracted, frustrated, unaware, and out of control. By contrast, strong mindfulness muscles make you more likely to feel focused, aware, grounded, and present. It's from a place of mindfulness that your cognitive abilities, judgment, and perspective are at their best. Through mindfulness, you can create new habits of thought.

Noticing Positives

My client Simon spent a lot of time on his phone. He scrolled first thing in the morning, on the commuter train, walking to work, during lunch, and while his family watched TV at night. When I asked him what good things had happened during his day, he couldn't come up with many examples. He was missing positive parts of life because he spent so much time mindlessly scrolling.

He decided to set some boundaries around his screen time and started practicing intentional mindfulness throughout his day. A few weeks later, when I asked him about the good things that had happened, he replied that he left the house feeling more cheerful because he intentionally paid more attention to his wife and kids at breakfast. When he walked to work without his earbuds in, he made eye contact and greeted more people. When he ate lunch outside, he noticed the trees, sun, and breeze. And when watching a movie with his family, he felt more connected and entertained.

You're more likely to feel down when your ability to be mindful of the good is weak. Are you missing out on positive emotions simply because you're not paying attention when you encounter good things?

Noticing Suffering

Another client, Emily, feels pretty good when she gets to work in the morning, but she often feels frustrated and cranky in the afternoon. Her productivity drops off, and her patience for others plummets. Her office has no windows, and she sometimes works through lunch without taking a break.

I invited her to be mindful of when her emotions were shifting and what conditions might be present in her body, mind, or environment. She noticed that her back and legs started getting stiff after about three hours, which made her antsy and impeded her ability to focus.

She decided to start taking a ten-minute walk before lunch and to eat by a window when she could. By being mindful of the triggers for her negative emotions, Emily was able to make a plan that supported her body and mind. It was so energizing for her to get up and go for a walk that she started regularly taking short walking breaks, which helped her maintain her energy and good mood throughout the day. If you struggle to recognize when you need to take care of yourself, you may feel anxious, frustrated, or stressed. Becoming more mindful of your basic needs leads to greater calm, peace, and positive energy.

Naming Feelings and Needs

The better you are at naming what you feel, the easier it is to navigate your emotions. For example, instead of saying, "I'm stressed," go further. Do you mean you're exhausted, depleted, worried, fearful, unconfident, anxious, overwhelmed, restless, confused, frustrated, angry, or something else? Exhaustion requires a different strategy than fear, overwhelm, confusion, or anger. Remember, emotions are signals about your needs. You feel negative emotions like "stress" when your needs are not being met. Having language to describe the nuances of your feelings expands your mindfulness. To help you identify what your emotions might be trying to communicate, below are some common universal needs, positive emotions, and negative emotions.

Universal Needs

Universal needs are exactly what they sound like: needs that we all have, regardless of where we live, where we come from, how we were raised, etc. I've adapted the following list from the work of Marshall Rosenberg in his book *Nonviolent Communication*:

- **Interdependence**—acceptance, belonging, equality, honesty, love, trust, friendship
- **Mental Health**—clarity, stimulation, understanding
- **Meaning**—challenge, growth, competence, contribution, hope
- **Peace**—beauty, ease, harmony, inspiration
- **Spirituality**—awareness, grace, gratitude, serving
- **Physical Health**—air, water, sunlight, rest, nourishment, movement, touch, comfort
- **Play**—adventure, fun, humor, joy, laughter, relaxation
- **Autonomy**—freedom, choice, self-empowerment, authenticity, space
- **Celebration of Life**—vitality, pleasure, self-respect, self-worth, purpose, passion
- **Connection**—affection, community, compassion, empathy, safety, feeling seen, feeling known

Common Positive Emotions

When your needs are met, you may feel affectionate, compassionate, warm, loving, confident, empowered, proud, safe, secure, curious, engrossed, stimulated, interested, excited, amazed, giddy, grateful, appreciative, hopeful, optimistic, awestruck, inspired, joyful, amused, happy, calm, centered, trusting, at peace, rejuvenated, restored, or revived.

Common Negative Emotions

When your needs are *not* being met, you may experience fear, dread, worry, hate, contempt, disgust, anger, outrage, resentment, aggravation, annoyance, frustration, irritation, restlessness, discomfort, unease, upset, burnout, depletion, exhaustion, disconnection, boredom, apathy, distraction, disinterest, embarrassment, shame, guilt, self-consciousness, pain, hurt, devastation, misery, heartbreak, loneliness, regret, sadness, depression, disappointment, discouragement, hopelessness, unhappiness, tension, anxiety, overwhelm, nervousness, stress, guardedness, helplessness, insecurity, envy, or jealousy.

Mapping Your Emotions

When you're armed with language to describe your feelings and needs, you can map your emotions and strategize how to transform them for the better. There are four steps to mapping your emotions.

- **Step 1:** Name the negative emotion you want to change.

- **Step** 2: Identify the unmet needs leading to that negative feeling.
- **Step** 3: Name the positive emotion you want to feel instead. This is your emotional goal!
- **Step** 4: Pick a strategy using Body Care, Behavior Care, or Mind Care to meet your needs.

Transforming Stress into Energy

Going back to the idea of stress, below is an example of mapping.

- **Step** 1: *I feel exhausted.*
- **Step** 2: *Why do I feel exhausted? My need for rest and relaxation isn't being met.*
- **Step** 3: *I want to feel refreshed, rejuvenated, and energized.*
- **Step** 4: *I can choose from different self-care options.*
  - **Body Care**: Get more sleep, eat healthier, or add exercise.
  - **Behavior Care**: Leave work on time, set boundaries, say no, or schedule quiet time.
  - **Mind Care**: Find more meaning in activities, and go from "have to" to "get to."

As you look at the options, which strategies jump out at you? Would you like to get better at setting boundaries and saying no so that you can get some sleep or improve your exercise?

Transforming Anger into Peace

Here's another example, this time involving anger:

- **Step** 1: *I feel angry.*
- **Step** 2: *Why do I feel angry? My need for order or fairness isn't being met.*
- **Step** 3: *I want to feel calm, loving, empathetic, and at peace.* (Note: These are different goals that may require different strategies.)
- **Step** 4: *I can choose from different self-care options.*
  - **Body Care**: Practice deep breathing, eat something if hangry, or go for a walk.
  - **Behavior Care**: Make a request rather than a demand, do something constructive, or apologize.
  - **Mind Care**: Empathize, accept, let go, appreciate, or forgive.

Transforming Fear into Confidence

For this last example, let's say you have an injured knee, poor balance, and a fear of falling. You feel anxious about walking because your need for safety is not being met, and your emotional goal is to feel confident while walking. From a strategy perspective, you can develop a feeling of safety and confidence through your body, behavior, or mind:

- **Body Care**: Build your physical strength, and practice balance to help you feel safe.
- **Behavior Care**: Use a cane, or go to the doctor to get assurances that walking is safe.
- **Mind Care**: Have hope and faith that your knee will hold up and get better.

Mental Muscle Memory

Here's a little secret: Body and behavior strategies help with confidence by changing how you think about your ability or situation. So ultimately, the work comes back to your mind. The mind both creates and fulfills psychological needs such as confidence, which explains the power of optimism.

Recall from the anatomy of thinking that 95 percent of your thinking is habitual. The goal of practicing mindfulness is not to eliminate autopilot and turn every thought into a conscious one. Instead, it's a way to help you make decisions in the moment that align with your most important values, as well as to train your subconscious patterns and develop your mental muscle memory.

Michael Jordan once made a free throw with his eyes closed during a basketball game. The first time I tried with my eyes closed, I shot the ball over the fence into the neighbor's yard. When you're first learning to shoot a basketball, you have to be mindful of every little detail. However, after lots of repetition, that movement pattern becomes so ingrained that you can literally make free throws with your eyes closed, as I eventually did!

Mindfulness and repetition train your brain, so that once you've developed a habit of gratitude or any other positive pattern, you can put it on autopilot for a while.

You don't have to be mindful every waking minute. You just have to pay attention long enough to intentionally choose where you want to go mentally and establish the new pattern of thinking.

Mindfulness is all about awareness. Without awareness, you can't be intentional about your actions—and without that perspective, it's harder to make wise choices. You can start by paying attention, on purpose, to the present moment. Then, use a mindfulness process like naming and mapping to provide clarity on your next step.

Mindfulness is often associated with meditation, because meditation is a great way to train your brain to be more focused and aware. But you can also use the Think, Speak, Write Mindset Workout Method to develop mindfulness.

MINDFULNESS MUSCLES: QUICK EMOTION GUIDE

- **Strong**: focus, awareness, grounding, presence, clarity
- **Weak**: distraction, unawareness, feeling of being rudderless, lack of control

---

Think, Speak, Write Mindset Workout Ideas

Strength Training: Positive Questions to Think About

- *What did I notice today?*
- *What am I noticing about my body?*
- *What am I noticing about others?*

Cardio: Positive Affirmations

- *I am present.*

- *I am aware.*
- *I act mindfully.*

Cardio: Conversation

Talk about something that you noticed or an insight you gained as a result of being mindful.

Stretching: Journal Prompts

- *How am I feeling at this moment?*
- *If I'm feeling good, what physical, social, or psychological needs are being met?*
- *If I'm feeling bad, what needs are not being met?*
- You can ponder any question to practice mindfulness.

Additional Exercises

The exercises below offer practice in being intentionally mindful. Simply pick something you want to pay attention to, and really focus on that thing. It could be people, nature, your body, or something else.

People-Watch

Sit in a public space and people-watch. Activate your inner Sherlock Holmes, tuning into what you see. Practice paying attention to friends, family, customers, or colleagues. Your ability to be mindful of what's going on with other people enhances your relationship abilities, leading to more empathy and connection and less frustration and anger.

Appreciate Nature

When going for a walk or sitting outside, practice paying attention to the natural world—sights, sounds, and smells. Look for the colors of the flowers and the sky, as well as the animals crawling or flying by. Listen for the rustling of leaves and chirping of birds. Stop to smell the roses, lilacs, or lavender. Nature can be very restorative and magnificent, and being mindful of it can evoke positive feelings like serenity, awe, connection, and gratitude.

Scan Your Body

One way you might practice being more mindful of your body is by using a mediation technique known as a body scan. Start by paying attention to your feet, and then work all the way up to your head, just observing the sensations.

Count Your Breaths

Spend time counting your breaths. This type of meditation can train your brain to focus.

Do a Digital Detox

Take a break from your phone. Doing a technology detox can heighten your other senses.

Spend Time with Yourself

Try some alone time. Spend time by yourself in contemplation, just you and your thoughts.

 UP YOUR OPTIMISM GAME: COACH'S CORNER 

Mastering meditation isn't the only way to become more mindful. Another route is simply to practice paying attention to what's happening, and then develop language to describe and communicate what you're noticing. If you're feeling stuck, a conversation with a trusted friend, mentor, or coach can help expand your perspective—others often see things you miss.

You can also use your vision muscles to tell your brain what you want it to notice, helping you become more mindful of the good. Building this skill will bring more joy and peace into your life.

TWELVE

SAVORING MUSCLES

*"Whether in a moment of peace
and quiet or exhilarating excitement,
savor every minute of every place."*
—LORRIE MORGAN

F MINDFULNESS IS AWARENESS OF POSITIVES, SAVOR-
ing is a way to magnify the intensity and duration of a positive experience. When you have a weakened digestive system,
it's harder to extract nutrients from food, creating a condition
in which you are well fed but undernourished. The same thing
can happen psychologically when your savoring muscles are
weaker. You may actually have enough positive "foods" in your
life, but you may not be extracting the positivity efficiently.

The opposite of savoring is minimizing or skipping over
good things. Have you ever received a compliment but
brushed it off as no big deal? Minimizing, downplaying, or dis-
crediting something good about yourself decreases the effect
of the positive words of affirmation. If you get into the habit

of downplaying everything good in your life, you'll feel fewer positive emotions—and at worst, you may create negative emotions.

When your savoring muscles are weak, you're more likely to feel that life is bland, dull, and tasteless. Emotionally, you might feel unfulfilled, apathetic, depressed, anxious, or insecure. But when your savoring muscles are strong, you'll feel more joy, happiness, and peace. So, savor all the good to spice up your life. Don't just swallow a compliment or spit it back out; roll it around on your tongue like a piece of chocolate and really taste it!

Magnifying Pleasure, Connection, Awe, and Pride

As a busy working mom, Kristen always has a lot going on in her world, and her mind jumps from thing to thing. When she learned to savor, she started pausing to actually taste and enjoy her coffee, which magnified the pleasure she experienced. When she encountered people, she took a deep breath and focused on their faces instead of being totally in her head. While walking the dog, she took time to notice the beauty of nature. And when someone said something nice to her, she really tried to hear it and let the compliment sink in.

As Kristen developed her savoring muscles, she was able to magnify the pleasure, connection, awe, and pride she felt throughout her day, and her life satisfaction increased. Without changing anything about your life, you could double or triple the positivity you experience, just by getting better at savoring.

SAVORING MUSCLES: QUICK EMOTION GUIDE

- **Strong**: joy, happiness, gratitude, and every other positive emotion
- **Weak**: depression, anxiety, lack of fulfillment, apathy, insecurity

Think, Speak, Write Mindset Workout Ideas

Strength Training: Positive Questions to Think About

- *What experiences do I want to savor and enjoy more deeply?*
- *How can savoring positively impact me?*

Cardio: Positive Affirmations

- *I soak in the good that's around me.*
- *I cherish time with family and friends.*
- *I savor pleasant moments.*

Cardio: Conversation

Tell someone about something that you enjoyed and savored.

Stretching: Journal Prompts

- *What did I savor today?*
- *What good experiences were really worth savoring?*

Additional Exercises

The Mindful Pause

When you experience something positive, pay attention. Pause for a moment to soak it in. You can develop your savoring muscles by picking a specific moment to pause during. It could be a cup of coffee, the fresh air, the look on your kid's face, or anything else that gives you joy. By being present to the positive experience as it's happening, you can magnify its effect.

The One-Minute Hug: Savoring Love and Connection

Hugs can become habits. You may give them on autopilot when you greet a loved one, but you can use mindfulness to savor the love and connection. For this exercise, you should tell the other person your intention and ask permission—otherwise, you might freak out Grandpa if you just start hanging on him for a full minute.

Maybe it's a weekly routine with a spouse, parent, or child. Maybe it's something you suggest when you haven't seen a friend or family member for a long time. There's nothing wrong with a quick side hug, but a good, full hug can really boost feelings of love, connection, belonging, and gratitude. So, squeeze your peeps and hold them tight.

 UP YOUR OPTIMISM GAME: COACH'S CORNER 

In the age of smartphones and constant notifications, many of us are training our minds to jump from thing to thing, looking for the next sugar high before we've even swallowed the food we're eating. But by strengthening your ability to savor the good that is already happening in your life, you'll feel more joy, happiness, and contentment.

You don't have to linger on everything; just choose a few key moments throughout the day that amplify the positivity you feel.

THIRTEEN

CELEBRATION AND APPRECIATION MUSCLES

*"The more you praise and celebrate your life,
the more there is in life to celebrate."*
—OPRAH WINFREY

S A KID, I HAD SOME EPIC BIRTHDAY PARTIES, including the infamous Minnie and Mickey Mouse cakes that left my younger sister covered in black frosting. Because we both have December birthdays, our parents went out of the way to really celebrate our special days. But as I got older, my birthday started blending into Christmas, final exams, and end-of-year work. My sophomore year of college, I had a physics final at 6:00 p.m. on the Friday of my birthday. Afterward, my best friends still took me to Pizzeria Uno in Kenmore Square to get a Chicago Classic pizza, but that's the day my birthday celebration muscles got a whole lot weaker, because it felt like just another day.

The minute we stop celebrating, our joy plummets. Celebration is a way to appreciate the best moments of life and share them with others, and it's related to the ideas of mindfulness and savoring. When your celebration muscles are strong, you'll feel more joy, happiness, pride, excitement, hope, and connection. However, the opposite of appreciating and celebrating is criticizing, complaining, and blaming, which may lead you to feel depressed, hopeless, discouraged, frustrated, angry, or disconnected.

To build up your celebration muscles, you don't have to jump, shout, and throw a party. Remember the key of *heartfelt*. There can be quiet moments alone or with a dear friend that help you celebrate yourself, others, and the good in life.

Celebrating Our Best

In order to celebrate something, you first have to notice and appreciate it. Appreciative inquiry is all about celebrating our best. Two classic appreciative inquiries are "What went well?" and "What's going well?" For instance, when you look back over the last year, what went well in your social life, work life, or personal life (e.g., birthdays, successes, or fond memories)?

Most of us are trained to be critical. We automatically focus on what goes wrong, which makes us feel anxious, frustrated, or not good enough. Being critical may help us learn from our mistakes, but success also leaves clues. It can be just as valuable as constructive criticism to ask, "What went right?" Practicing appreciation helps to balance out an overly critical mind.

Potato, Potahto, Tomato, Tomahto

Appreciation and gratitude are cousins. They sound similar and often go together. It's okay if you use the terms interchangeably, but below is a sample of how they differ slightly.

- **Gratitude**: *I'm grateful for my job. I'm grateful for my boss. I'm grateful for my salary.*
- **Appreciation**: *What went well? We finished on time, the host was great, and the food was amazing.*
- **Self-Appreciation**: *I am creative and brave, and my hard work has helped me to be successful.*

Here's another example:

- **Gratitude**: *I'm grateful for my son.*
- **Appreciation**: *What went well? My son made the honor roll and the track team.*
- **Appreciation of Others**: *My son showed initiative, focus, and determination this year.*

Like life, emotions are nuanced and interconnected. You can be grateful for what you appreciate. Appreciation is acknowledging and celebrating the goodness, while gratitude is being thankful for the goodness. The muscle names are there to help you navigate your thoughts and experiences, not set some rigid box that everything has to fit inside perfectly. So, apply your wisdom to use the terms as you see fit.

Cheer On and Celebrate Others

In sports, there is something known as the "home court advantage." When we play in front of people who are cheering us on, we perform better. My mom had been a cheerleader in high school, and she made all of my basketball games home games. I could always count on her to shout words of encouragement from the stands. As a teenager, I sometimes got embarrassed, because she was often louder than everyone else put together—but in retrospect, I am so grateful for her cheers.

It's amazing what we can do when people cheer us on, and we can give that same gift to others, strengthening our celebration and appreciation of them. So, cheer for others and celebrate their successes. It doesn't have to be anything big. It could be a few words of affirmation like "congrats," "well done," or "you got this"—or a gesture like a smile, thumbs-up, or high five. Celebrating connects us with others and fills us with positive emotions. So, the next time you cheer for someone, watch what happens to them, and then notice what happens in you. And remember to also cheer for and celebrate yourself!

CELEBRATION AND APPRECIATION MUSCLES: QUICK EMOTION GUIDE

- **Strong:** joy, happiness, excitement, pride, hope, connection
- **Weak:** depression, discouragement, feelings of not being or having enough, anger, boredom, disconnection

Think, Speak, Write Mindset Workout Ideas

Strength Training: Positive Questions to Think About

- *What went well?*
- *What's going well?*

Cardio: Positive Affirmations

- *I celebrate good things.*
- *I cheer for myself and others.*
- *I celebrate small wins each day.*

Cardio: Conversation

Tell someone about what went well or what's going well. Ask them to share what's going well in their life.

Stretching: Journal Prompts

Ask these questions about your work life, your home life, your personal experience, or the state of the world:

- *What went well?*
- *What's going well?*
- *What's something worth celebrating?*

Additional Exercises

Create a Celebration Ritual

Pick a small milestone or win to celebrate. When you hit ten thousand steps, give yourself a high five. Every Friday when you get home, do a happy dance. Whenever you take a step toward a goal, say to yourself, *Good work*. Celebrating small wins reinforces the behavior and adds positivity.

Throw a Party

Birthdays, anniversaries, and holidays are all great occasions to throw a party, but you can make up any reason to get together. During your gathering, you can go around the room and ask everyone to share what went well so that you can cheer and celebrate with them.

Play Some Tunes

Music can create a mood. So, fire up your favorite songs and get your groove on. I recommend listening to "Celebration" by Kool & the Gang on repeat!

 **UP YOUR OPTIMISM GAME: COACH'S CORNER**

Criticism is a survival mechanism related to our fight-or-flight response. It helps us attack or protect, and it riles up negative emotions like anger or fear to motivate us. Being critical is a necessary skill, but an overly critical mind is dominated by negative emotions.

If you consistently lift your appreciation dumbbells, you can tamp down the negative emotions that flow from criticism, instead building more joy, harmony, and peace. What went well? What's going well? What are you doing well? What are others doing well? What's worth celebrating?

Get those appreciation reps in to celebrate life, yourself, and others.

FOURTEEN

JOY MUSCLES

Beauty is whatever gives joy.
—EDNA ST. VINCENT MILLAY

A MEMORY FROM HER OLDEST DAUGHTER'S FIFTH birthday party popped up on Kristen's social media feed. She clicked on the video and started smiling. After opening a gift, her five- and two-year-old daughters started playing with the box and wrapping paper and were cracking themselves up. It was total cuteness and pure joy.

One of the best feelings you can have is joy flowing through your soul, and Kristen listed joy as one of her top emotional goals. For inspiration, she looked to her daughters, who both have really strong joy muscles. In fact, joy is something many adults could learn from kids.

When we're younger, our joy muscles tend to be stronger, and when injured, they heal quickly. However, as we get older, life constantly tests our joy with breakups, sickness, money challenges, and loss of loved ones. All the injuries can cause us to stop using our joy. Then, months or years later, we wake up one day with weak and flabby joy muscles.

When your joy muscles are weak, it's harder to feel pleasure, and you're more likely to feel depression, misery, sadness, and displeasure with all things around you. But fortunately, you can build your joy back up! Strong gratitude muscles help your joy muscles work better, allowing you to feel more enjoyment, happiness, bliss, and pleasure. In that state of mind, you'll have an easy smile and effortless laugh, and even little things will give you a sense of delight and cheer.

Giving Yourself Permission

My best friends have trained their dog to sit and wait for treats. They put one on the ground and say, "Wait," and she patiently waits with longing eyes. She won't go after the treats until they say, "It's okay." And as soon as they give her permission...*nom nom nom*.

Behavioral anhedonia is a term used to describe when someone engages in behavior that leads them to avoid pleasure. Sometimes, you might tell yourself a story that makes you feel bad for feeling good. If you feel guilty or shameful for feeling pleasure, you'll find ways to avoid it. This can happen when mourning any kind of loss. When you break up with someone, lose your job, or lose a loved one, sadness is a normal response. It signals that something important has been lost. But sometimes, we hold on to sadness as a sign of respect for the loss. We feel guilty when we start feeling good again, which reinforces a negative coping strategy.

After my client Patricia's mother died, for instance, she felt great sadness. But she didn't want to get over it too quickly. In her mind, if she wasn't sad, it would diminish the importance of her loss. She started to identify sadness as a sign of her love—to show she loved her mother, she had to keep feeling sad. This is a common thinking trap that stops people from seeking joy and pleasure after loss.

When I went through a heartbreaking divorce, I told myself that I would mourn for a year, as proof to myself that the relationship was meaningful and important. It was easily the most depressing year of my life. On top of the shame, guilt, loss, isolation, and pain, I forbade myself to even consider another relationship, which exacerbated the isolation and depression. My story trapped me in a negative space, and my behavior reinforced it. Looking back, I wish I had asked for help and talked more with my friends and family about what I was going through. But hey, I'm a guy, and often guys don't ask for help—we just suffer in silence. Lesson learned.

If you're trying to bounce back and reclaim your joy, the first thing you have to do is give yourself permission to feel it. Tell yourself it's okay to heal, grow, move on, laugh, live, love, feel good, and be joyful. And it's also okay to ask for help if you need it.

Don't Dampen Your Joy

Another limiting mindset is the tendency to dampen your joy and exuberance when other people around you are struggling. You might think, *I don't want to make them feel bad by saying that I'm doing great.* But by dimming your light, are you actually helping them? Misery loves company, but so does joy. Instead of turning down your light, turn it up as a bright beacon for others. If everyone dulls their light, the world will be a darker place. So, give yourself permission to shine your brightest.

The concept of permission applies to every positive emotion. If you define experiencing a positive emotion as a bad thing, you will either consciously or subconsciously avoid that emotion. In addition to joy, this dynamic also commonly happens with pride, satisfaction, love, hope, and faith.

Give yourself permission to hope, to feel proud, and to love. Seek pleasure. Seek bliss. Seek joy!

Major Exercise: Beautiful Day

In addition to the Strengths Résumé and Gratitude Letter, the Beautiful Day is the third major exercise of the six-week Optimism Challenge. I first learned of this exercise from the father of positive psychology, Martin Seligman. Simply plan a day (or half day) with a specific focus on using your strengths, pursuing your interests, or connecting with the most important people in your life.

If you had four to eight hours to devote to feeling joyful, what activities would you plan? Where would you go? Who would you spend time with? Life can get so busy that we forget to exercise our joy, but periodically planning a Beautiful Day can keep those muscles strong.

For me, Beautiful Days often include five things: movement, time outdoors, good food, great people, and board games. I also like creative projects, movies, and sporting events. Some of my Beautiful Days are solo days—I take a trip to the beach, get a nice lunch, and just relax. Sometimes it's visiting friends, going for a walk, and playing games. Sometimes it's going to church, brunch, and the movies with Mom.

The beautiful thing about the Beautiful Day exercise is that whatever gives you joy is fair game. So, plan days around the things that make you feel the most joyful.

JOY MUSCLES: QUICK EMOTION GUIDE

- **Strong**: enjoyment, happiness, bliss, pleasure
- **Weak**: depression, displeasure, misery, sadness

Think, Speak, Write Mindset Workout Ideas

Strength Training: Positive Questions to Think About

- What brings you joy?
- What was a joyful moment of your life?

Cardio: Positive Affirmations

- *I seek joy.*
- *I welcome joy into my life.*
- *I give myself permission to shine.*

Cardio: Conversation

Tell someone about something that brings you joy, or talk about a joyful moment.

Stretching: Journal Prompts

- *What made me smile today?*
- *Who or what added some joy to my day?*
- Write about a joyful memory.

Additional Exercises

Smile!

Practice smiling in the mirror for thirty to sixty seconds. Smiling can trigger your brain to release chemicals that help you feel happier and less stressed.

Behave Like a Child

Sing, dance, play, and laugh. Do what brings you joy.

 **UP YOUR OPTIMISM GAME: COACH'S CORNER** 

I know there may be hard things in your life right now, and it's okay to feel bad. But I want to remind you that it's also okay to feel joyful, even when everything isn't perfect.

Sometimes, we wait for the perfect moment to feel good. We think to ourselves, *I'll feel joyful when…I have a lot of money, there is no crime or injustice, and all my family is healthy and happy.* However, the perfect time never comes, and we talk ourselves into staying miserable.

However, if you look at your past moments of joy, you'll likely find that many things weren't perfect at the time—yet you still felt joy, because it's more about your focus and your story than your circumstances.

So, you don't have to wait to be joyful! Your body doesn't have to be perfect. Your life doesn't have to be perfect. The world doesn't have to be perfect. Choosing joy isn't always easy, but as you up your optimism game, you'll see more light—even on dark days.

FIFTEEN

HUMOR AND FUN MUSCLES

"Comedy is acting out optimism."
—ROBIN WILLIAMS

MY PARENTS SEPARATED WHEN I WAS NINE, SO I had to grow up fast. By age ten, I had chores, a key to the house, and big brother responsibilities. In fifth grade, I remember standing on the front porch with a key around my neck and a piece of chocolate in my hand, when I proclaimed, "I'm going to work hard and do well in school, so when I grow up, my family won't have to worry about money." That's when my seriousness muscles grabbed the wheel and my fun muscles took a back seat.

As a teenager, when my cousins played and horsed around, I was on the sidelines watching the fun and telling them to be careful. I took everything they said literally, and they often made fun of me for not getting their jokes. I did all my homework and followed the rules.

School can beat the fun out of us with all the rules and expectations, and in that setting, seriousness can help us "succeed." During college, I studied ahead instead of going to parties, and I worked instead of playing around. I love learning, so being a nerd was fun in a way, but the pursuit of academic excellence made me even more serious. My analytical mind took over: *How exactly does everything work? I have to earn straight A's and get everything right!* Seriousness was the seed that grew into the perfectionism and neuroticism that many of my friends and I suffered from as adults.

Our seriousness was an asset to employers, because we obsessed over solving problems. I got used to grinding, and achievement was "fun," so I often worked seven days a week to reach goals. Work became my identity, and fun was a luxury I couldn't afford. As a result, I kept burning myself out.

A turning point came in my late thirties during a conversation with my coaching mentor. I was very serious about getting results, and after watching me coach someone, my mentor invited me to integrate more playfulness into my coaching style. She said, "Charles, coaching is serious business, but it doesn't have to be the business of seriousness."

As much as seriousness could sometimes be an asset, I noticed that when I leaned into fun and play, clients got better results. Sure, diabetes and joint pain are serious issues, but to solve them through lifestyle changes, we have to enjoy the process. As my humor muscles grew, my coaching conversations got lighter and more enjoyable. Clients started tapping into their inner children in a way that made them playful and energized! Noticing how fun helped clients, I continued to lighten up and not take myself or life so seriously, and my joy grew.

Your humor muscles are next to your joy muscles, and they generate similar emotions. When your humor and fun muscles are strong, you're more likely to feel happy, joyful, playful, and light. The opposite of humor and fun is seriousness. When your fun muscles are weak, everything feels heavier, and you're more likely to feel sad, exhausted, and frustrated. As with any muscle, your fun muscles get weaker if you don't use them.

Adulting often weakens our fun muscles because we have to deal with so many serious issues. With the weight of the world on our shoulders, it can be hard to stand tall. But stronger humor and fun muscles can keep you joyful and light. Life can be serious business, but it doesn't have to be the business of seriousness.

Lighten Up, Buttercup

Inspired by Patch Adams, the famous physician comedian, Joe's physician Dr. Dave believes laughter is such good medicine that he prescribes it to his patients to help with emotional symptoms like depression, anxiety, and stress, as well as physical conditions like chronic pain and high blood pressure. The pressure of Joe's job had been weighing on him, and he became so serious that he rarely smiled. Dr. Dave and I both encouraged Joe to lean into his strength of humor to improve his physical and mental health. To work out his humor muscles, Joe decided to start meetings by telling a joke. Not only was the laughter good for him, his team also began looking forward to his jokes.

During our sessions, Joe even had jokes for me. "Charles," he said, "what do you call a dog who meditates?"

I had no idea.

"Aware wolf."

That's funny.

"I thought you'd appreciate that one, Coach," he told me.

Humor played an important role in helping Joe combat his stress. A little laughter can also be great for *your* body, mind, and soul, so make sure you get your daily dose.

HUMOR MUSCLES: QUICK EMOTION GUIDE

- **Strong**: joy, happiness, playfulness, delight, sense of lightness
- **Weak**: misery, somberness, depression, seriousness, heaviness

---

Think, Speak, Write Mindset Workout Ideas

Strength Training: Positive Questions to Think About

- *How can I add humor and fun to my days?*
- *What was a really funny moment?*

Cardio: Positive Affirmations

- *Laughter is medicine.*
- *I seek fun.*
- *Smiling is my favorite activity.*

Cardio: Conversation

Tell someone a funny story or joke.

Stretching: Journal Prompts

- *What are my top three to five go-to fun activities?*
- *Who or what made me laugh today?*

Additional Exercises

You already know how to have fun...I hope! Still, here are some additional ideas.

Make Time for Fun

Do something amusing. Work and caregiving are important, but also schedule time for fun.

Find Your Inner Comedian

Practice cultivating and unleashing your humor. Take an improv class, or write your own stand-up comedy routine. You can also text someone a joke every day for a week or just read jokes online for the fun of it.

Keep It Light

Instead of serious content like educational podcasts, audiobooks, and news shows, listen to more comedy and watch funny animal videos. When I'm cooking or walking outside, I often listen to stand-up comedy, and my friends say I've gotten funnier.

 **UP YOUR OPTIMISM GAME: COACH'S CORNER** 

Living in Boston, I meet a lot of serious people. With over fifty colleges in the greater Boston area and more than one hundred statewide, Massachusetts is a hub for education. Many of us have traveled thousands of miles from home to pursue growth, so we're serious about being successful. Seriousness benefits our education and career—but not always our mental health.

It's okay if you're a serious person, but don't let it stop you from having a little fun. You don't have to be a stand-up comedian. Just try making time for fun, and practice being more playful so that you and those around you experience more joy and happiness.

SIXTEEN

LOVE MUSCLES

*"And now these three remain: faith, hope,
and love—but the greatest of these is love."*
—1 CORINTHIANS 13:13 (NIV)

LOVE IS A POWERFUL EMOTION! IT INSPIRES US, challenges us, gives us purpose, and makes life meaningful. Love attracts! The ultimate power of love lies in building and strengthening connection. The stronger your love muscles, the more joyful, energized, ecstatic, connected, secure, and peaceful you'll feel.

The opposite of love is hate. Hate weakens or completely severs connection. When your hate muscles flex, you will repel others, leading to more physical and emotional isolation—and you can't live a meaningful life without quality relationships. When your love muscles are weak, you're more likely to feel anger, frustration, sadness, loneliness, anxiety, and depression. Those negative feelings can have real health consequences;

chronic anger, for instance, is associated with heart problems, headaches, and digestive problems. Strengthening your love muscles can heal your body, mind, and soul.

I acknowledge that others' actions can influence your experience of love, but since a key to inner peace and empowerment is focusing on what *you* can control, I want to talk to you about strengthening your love muscles through how you give, receive, perceive, and ask for love.

Showing Love With the Five Love Languages

Jaylen was thirty when I first met him, and his biggest source of stress and anxiety was his fear that he would never find true love, get married, and have a family of his own. He grew up in a tough neighborhood with his single mom, and because he didn't have many great relationship role models, he struggled to maintain a serious relationship for more than six months at a time. After hearing his relationship frustrations, I suggested he pick up a copy of *The Five Love Languages: Singles Edition* by Gary Chapman.

According to Chapman, there are five ways you can express and receive love:

1. Words of Affirmation
2. Acts of Service
3. Gifts
4. Quality Time
5. Physical Touch

Jaylen decided physical touch was his primary love language, because physical chemistry had always been important to him in a relationship. He realized he'd been clueless when it came to dating and showing love. He hadn't been good at complimenting or giving gifts, and maybe that was why his relationships fizzled out. After reflecting on love languages, he began communicating online with a woman named Keisha. Having chatted for several weeks, they agreed to meet up. Armed with this new information, Jaylen felt optimistic and confident.

Being Open to Accepting and Receiving Love

Keisha had gotten married right out of college, but after a traumatic divorce, she'd been single for over eight years. She tried to date, but her fear of getting hurt again led her to keep potential boyfriends at a distance. Through a friend from yoga class, she met a love and relationship coach who worked with her on becoming more open to receiving love. One of the biggest lessons Keisha learned is that love is risky—but so is everything else in life. She needed the courage to be vulnerable and open up to the possibility that things would work out.

As Keisha waited for Jaylen to arrive, she repeated a mantra to herself: *I am ready to let love in.* Jaylen came around the corner with a big cheesy smile and a bouquet of flowers. "Thank you—these are beautiful," Keisha said. "No one's ever brought me flowers on a first date."

"They're not as pretty as you, but they're a close second," he replied.

Instead of blocking or dampening the kindness, Keisha graciously received the compliments and allowed the love in. Jaylen noticed how nice it felt expressing his emotions with gifts and words. The date felt like it could be the start of something good.

Over the first few months of dating, Jaylen continued practicing showing love in multiple ways, and he and Keisha grew closer. At the one-year mark, Jaylen felt like he'd found the person he wanted to spend the rest of his life with, and Keisha felt the same.

Whether it's an intimate relationship, a close family relationship, or a work relationship, you can increase your level of connection to others by showing love in different ways. And when you are on the receiving end, it's important to let love in.

Recognizing Love and Kindness

Another client, Molly, had been married to her husband, Chris, for five years. They had three-year-old twin sons. In the beginning of their marriage, Molly was head over heels in love, but after getting swept up in parenthood, she felt stressed, overwhelmed, and underappreciated. She'd become increasingly disillusioned with her relationship and felt constant frustration toward her husband.

I empathized and suggested that she could use the five love languages as a way to strengthen her appreciation of others muscles, specifically with Chris. She agreed and started intentionally trying to find the ways that Chris was showing love. As she did so, she started noticing more love coming her way. She told me that because they were in a different phase of life, the acts of love looked different, which made it harder for her to recognize at first.

"He used to buy me flowers, take me to dinner, and plan day trips," she said. "Now, he makes sure the fridge is stocked with my favorite yogurt. He is so quiet in the morning so that he doesn't wake me up, and he sometimes rubs my shoulders when we watch TV. I was taking all the little things for granted."

People will show you love and kindness in many different ways, but if you don't perceive those efforts, you won't experience them. To enhance your feelings of happiness and connection, put on your love lenses and look for the ways people are showing you love and kindness.

Asking for Love: Requests vs. Demands

While Molly started feeling more love when she got better at recognizing it, we didn't stop there. There were things she was missing and wanted to share with Chris, so I introduced her to Marshall Rosenberg's concept of Nonviolent Communication (NVC), also known as Compassionate Communication, which I described in Chapter 11.

One of the tenets of NVC is that making requests is a more compassionate way to communicate your needs than making demands. When you make a request and communicate your needs in a loving and compassionate way, it increases the chances that your needs will be met. So instead of demanding that Chris change "or else," Molly and I worked to define her needs and the requests she wanted to make. The secret to making a nonviolent request is that you have to be okay if the other person says no or does not comply; otherwise, it's a demand.

Molly missed going out to dinner with just the two of them, so she made a request that they work together to find more opportunities to get some quality alone time outside of the house. As it turned out, Chris also missed those dinner dates, and his mom had been begging to see the kids more often. Friday date night was born, and it became an anchor of love and connection for their relationship.

It's okay to ask people to support you and show you love and kindness in ways that really make you feel good. You can ask in a harsh, demanding way or in a loving, honest way. Getting better at asking for love in a compassionate way will increase the amount of love that comes back to you.

Relationships can be complicated, so I know this strategy won't solve all your relationship challenges. But keep this in mind: You *can* feel more love and connection if you get better at perceiving, receiving, giving, and asking for love.

LOVE MUSCLES: QUICK EMOTION GUIDE

- **Strong**: devotion, joy, energy, connection, affection, belonging, peace
- **Weak**: hate, anger, frustration, sadness, loneliness, anxiety, depression

Think, Speak, Write Mindset Workout Ideas

Strength Training: Positive Questions to Think About

- *Who do I love and value?*
- *What acts of love and kindness have I received?*
- *What acts of love and kindness have I expressed?*

Cardio: Positive Affirmations

- *I value love.*
- *I welcome love into my life.*
- *I am grateful for all the love and kindness I receive.*

Cardio: Conversation

Tell someone that you love them and share why.

Stretching: Journal Prompts

Regularly writing about when you express and receive love will heighten your ability to notice and experience love, so make sure to stretch your love muscles:

- Write a story about a person you love and why you love them.
- Journal one to three moments when you received or expressed love during the day.

Additional Exercises

Express Love via the Five Love Languages

You may already be good at expressing love, and with some additional mindfulness and savoring, you can magnify the positive effects. Focus on specific relationships or on express-ing love and kindness in general to family, friends, and cowork-ers. Pick expressions you are already good at, like giving gifts, or challenge yourself to grow in a new area. Below are a few ideas.

- **Words of Affirmation**: Say "I love you" to a loved one every day, or offer other words of affirmation to someone daily.
- **Acts of Service**: Find ways to be of service every day. Hold doors, lend a helping hand, or find other ways to contribute. Perform random acts of kindness or volunteer.
- **Gifts**: Give small gifts—whatever speaks to your heart.
- **Quality Time and Quality Activities**: Take a break from technology when you're with your peeps. Play a board game, read to your kids, or just sit and talk without distractions. Be intentional about doing quality activities and spending quality time with your loved ones.
- **Physical Touch**: Get in your hugs, handshakes, high fives, cuddles, and back rubs.

Practice Requesting Love and Support

If you are a people pleaser who tends to put others' needs above your own to the point that you get resentful, try prac-ticing loving and compassionate communication by making nonviolent requests.

Give Yourself Permission to Love

Practice incorporating this mindset shift by repeating to your-self, *I give myself permission to love.*

 **UP YOUR OPTIMISM GAME: COACH'S CORNER** 

Love is a great mental health elixir. It decreases anger, loneliness, and depression and increases joy, peace, and connection. While the examples in this chapter mostly focus on romantic partnership love, the ideas can be used in any relationship. You can work to develop more love with your parents, children, siblings, and friends—and even random people you encounter over the course of your day. Love is love.

We all need love, so spend some time creating a loving mindset. Then, put that mindset into practice by perceiving, receiving, asking for, and giving love.

SEVENTEEN

SELF-COMPASSION AND SELF-LOVE MUSCLES

*"If your compassion does not
include yourself, it is incomplete."*
—JACK KORNFIELD

A S HER OWN WORST CRITIC, IT WAS HARDER FOR Kristen to love herself than to love other people. I asked her to tell me about the people she loved the most, and she named her mom, husband, and daughters. Then I asked if any of them were perfect.

Kristen laughed and said, "Absolutely not."

I reflected, "So in your closest relationships, perfection isn't a requirement for you to love someone."

She paused, then said, "Hmm, I'm holding myself to a different standard than everyone else. I guess I don't have to be perfect in order to love myself."

Bingo! To be human means to be flawed, and everyone is worthy of love—including you.

Self-compassion refers to your ability to treat yourself with the same kindness, patience, and grace that you offer others. Self-love unlocks many positive emotions. Your self-compassion muscles work with your self-appreciation muscles to help you feel loved, supported, happy, secure, grounded, connected, and at peace with yourself. From a behavioral perspective, when you're good at loving yourself, you'll be better at setting and maintaining personal boundaries, fostering positive relationships, engaging in self-care activities, and pursuing your dreams.

The opposites of self-compassion and self-love are self-cruelty and self-hate. When your self-love muscles are weak, you're more likely to feel depression, anxiety, unworthiness, frustration, shame, and guilt. You might always put others' needs ahead of your own, push off your dreams, become lax in taking care of yourself, and enter into or tolerate more negative relationships. But you can build up your self-love muscles so that you are your own best friend.

Earning Her Master's in Self-Compassion

Kristen really wanted to strengthen these muscles, so we discussed some strategies during a coaching session. One of the ways to get better at self-love is to disentangle success and perfection from being worthy of love.

This can be challenging at first, because society most often praises us for our accomplishments: "Wow, you got an A." "Wow, you're pretty." "Wow, you won the game." If you have been successful in any area and have received praise for that success, it's easy to start connecting your worthiness with what you do and achieve instead of with who you *are*, imperfections and all.

The truth is, you are worthy of love and kindness simply because you are a part of the human family. If you only send love to yourself when you're perfect or accomplish something amazing, your self-love muscles will atrophy. Remember, two things can be true at the same time: You can make mistakes and still love yourself.

Motivation by Criticism and Shame: Does It Work?

One reason Kristen was so self-critical was that she worried she'd slack off and not be motivated if she didn't constantly stay vigilant about her mistakes and shortcomings. American culture heavily relies on criticism and shame as strategies to motivate people to change. Parents, teachers, sports coaches, and bosses yell at us. In this environment, it's easy to believe that yelling at yourself is the best way to meet your full potential.

However, this belief only amplifies your inner critic. Just like parents and teachers, your inner critic means well. It's trying to guide you to avoid mistakes or improve performance, but the inner critic is usually not the best coach.

On rare occasions, proving haters wrong might drive you to succeed, but more often, criticism completely quashes your motivation. When you think about your proudest accomplishments in life, you'll probably notice that love and support provided the best fuel. So, if you're trying to motivate yourself to change, tell your inner critic you're hiring a new coach.

Kristen's Self-Love Workout

Because this concept was so important for Kristen, I asked her if she wanted me to lead her through a quick Mindset Workout focused on self-love, and she agreed. I asked her to close her eyes and place both hands over her heart. I cued her to begin by taking three deep breaths. Then, she repeated the following affirmations out loud after me:

- *Perfection is not my standard for worthiness of love.*
- *My friends have flaws, and I love them.*
- *My family makes mistakes, and I love them.*
- *My people are imperfect, and I love them anyway.*
- *Even though I am imperfect, I deeply and completely love and accept myself.*
- *Even though I make mistakes, I deeply and completely love and accept myself.*
- *Even though I am flawed, I am worthy of love and kindness.*
- *I am worthy of self-love.*
- *I am worthy of self-kindness.*
- *I am worthy of self-forgiveness.*
- *I send love to me.*

After our five-minute workout, Kristen wiped a tear from her cheek and said, "I need to keep practicing these." She remembered how much work it took to earn her master's degree, so she knew it would take time to master self-compassion as well. Fortunately, she believes she's worth the investment. You too can learn to be more self-compassionate so that you feel loved, supported, and at peace with yourself.

SELF-COMPASSION AND SELF-LOVE MUSCLES: QUICK EMOTION GUIDE

- **Strong**: love, support, happiness, self-assurance, connection to self, peace with self
- **Weak**: anxiety, depression, unworthiness, frustration, shame, guilt

---

Think, Speak, Write Mindset Workout Ideas

Strength Training: Positive Questions to Think About

- *What is possible if I get better at loving myself more?*
- *How can I show myself love?*

Cardio: Positive Affirmations

To extend love to yourself, place one or both hands over your heart when repeating affirmations:

- *I love you.*
- *I accept you.*
- *I forgive you.*
- *You are worthy of my love.*

Cardio: Conversation

Tell someone about a positive thing that happened as a result of loving yourself more.

Stretching: Journal Prompts

- *How have I shown myself love in thought or action?*
- *How am I growing or making an impact as a result of being more self-compassionate?*

Additional Exercises

Self-Care and Self-Love Routines (Daily, Weekly, or Monthly)

Any act of self-care is also an act of self-love. You don't have to commit to anything extreme, but you might find that developing daily, weekly, or monthly self-care routines helps you to more consistently show love to yourself and your body.

Any activity counts, as long as you interpret it as an act you are doing for yourself. Through your mind, you can experience more self-love by interpreting daily tasks as acts of self-care. Maybe reading, taking a bath, working out, eating a delicious meal, watching movies, being in nature, or connecting with your community are part of your self-love routine.

Just like Molly started feeling more love when she looked for the ways her husband showed her love, you can feel more love by noticing the ways you already show *yourself* love.

Best Friend Letter

Write a letter to yourself as if you were writing to your best friend. You can write about challenging times or celebratory occasions. When you write to yourself, it can serve to give you distance from the situation. With this added distance, it's easier to observe, so your compassion may flow more easily toward yourself through writing.

 **UP YOUR OPTIMISM GAME: COACH'S CORNER** 

To paraphrase Whitney Houston, self-love is the "greatest love of all." We can be surrounded by family and friends who love us, but if we don't love ourselves, we'll still feel sad, depressed, ashamed, and unworthy. Loving yourself doesn't mean you don't try to improve; it just acknowledges that you are human and worthy of self-love, regardless of your performance and imperfections.

If you are your own worst critic, don't lose hope: You can learn to be your own best friend. When you treat yourself with the same love and kindness that you show your friends, your emotional world will transform, and you'll feel more loved, supported, and at peace with yourself. So, remember to send love to *you*.

EIGHTEEN

CONFIDENCE MUSCLES

"Believe in yourself! Have faith in your abilities! Without a humble but reasonable confidence in your own powers you cannot be successful or happy."
—NORMAN VINCENT PEALE

CONFIDENCE CAN COME FROM YOUR FOCUS AND story. Self-appreciation and self-compassion work with your confidence muscles to help you feel composed, self-assured, hopeful, and up for a challenge. But when your confidence muscles are weak, you'll tend to feel insecure, anxious, doubtful, hopeless, and depressed.

Low confidence can keep you stuck in a negative emotional cycle: You think you can't do something, which makes you depressed or anxious, so you never try. Because you never try, you never get a chance to grow your confidence, which keeps you stuck in the same place that makes you depressed or anxious. Fortunately, with some simple tweaks in focus, story, and behavior, you can beef up your confidence muscles—allowing you to eagerly pursue your goals and walk through life with a little more swag.

Do the Damn Thing: The Safe Experiment

When I was learning to drive a stick shift, a friend took me to an empty parking lot early in the morning when no one was around so that I could experiment in a safe environment. I continued to practice in parking lots until I felt confident enough to practice on the road.

Sometimes, the best way to improve confidence is to increase your skill by just doing the damn thing, with support in a safe space. When teaching kids, we usually start small to build up their confidence (with supports like training wheels or floaties), but as adults, we often put an unrealistic pressure on ourselves to be good at something before we've learned or practiced it. But if you get support and do the damn thing over and over, your skill and confidence will grow.

Looking Back: Mastery Experiences and Peak Moments

According to Albert Bandura's social cognitive theory, one source of self-efficacy (aka confidence) is mastery experiences. Nothing breeds confidence like success. Mastery experiences are successes, peak moments, or skills you've developed through practice and effort.

I've mentioned that I taught gross anatomy labs. At one point when I was in the lab, it hit me: If I can learn every bone and muscle, I can learn anything. And when I was faced with new challenges where my confidence was low, I'd remind myself of that mastery experience: *Charles, if you can learn anatomy, you can learn anything.*

Mastery experiences are evidence from your own life regarding what you are capable of. You can lean on that evidence as you attempt to grow in a familiar or new realm. What have you mastered in the past? What can your peak moments and past successes teach you about yourself? Strengthen your confidence muscles by consistently asking positive questions about your history.

Looking Forward: Faith and Confidence

Looking back on the past for mastery experiences is one of the most powerful ways to boost confidence, but you can also strengthen confidence by developing optimism about the future. In addition to vision, which we've already discussed, your confidence muscles work synergistically with your courage, hope, and faith muscles. We'll cover those muscles in more detail in future chapters, but for now, just be mindful that faith is necessary for confidence.

Additional Sources of Self-Efficacy

In addition to mastery experiences, Bandura states that your confidence is influenced by role models (vicarious experiences), positive conversations with yourself or someone else (verbal persuasion), and the state of your body. Finding a role model who's walked the path already can support your belief that you will also succeed. Positive conversations with a skilled coach or confidant can boost confidence. And your confidence will be higher when you put your body in a peak state of readiness through rest, nutrition, and movement.

Confidence comes from your optimism about your ability to achieve a goal. When you think, speak, and write about your successes and strengths, that positive focus will create a more confident mindset.

CONFIDENCE MUSCLES: QUICK EMOTION GUIDE

- **Strong**: composure, self-assurance, self-esteem, hope, faith, courage, preparedness
- **Weak**: insecurity, apprehension, hopelessness, doubt, anxiety, depression

---

Think, Speak, Write Mindset Workout Ideas

Strength Training: Positive Questions to Think About

- *When have I been successful at something in the past?*
- *What strengths do I have that I can leverage moving forward?*
- *What resources, people, places, or technology can I lean on for support?*

Cardio: Positive Affirmations

- *I am confident in my abilities.*
- *I am capable of growing.*
- *I can do this.*
- *I am _____.* (Fill in the blank with a strength you want to affirm, e.g., *smart, strong, persistent.*)

Cardio: Conversation

Talk with someone about your successes and strengths.

Stretching: Journal Prompts

- Write about a mastery experience, past success, or peak moment.
- Write about your strengths in action, which relates to self-appreciation.

Additional Exercises

The Dress Rehearsal: Positive Future Visualization

You can build confidence through a mental dress rehearsal where you imagine doing well. For instance, if you feel nervous about an upcoming presentation, sit or stand in a posture that reflects confidence, and then mentally visualize the steps you'll take to succeed. Imagine the audience responding well. Imagine yourself doing well.

Visualization works both ways; mentally rehearsing things going badly will increase fear and worry. But if you practice seeing yourself succeed, it will be easier for you to step onto that stage and shine.

The Safe Experiment: Do the Damn Thing

Find support and practice in a safe environment to develop your skill.

Two-Minute Power Posing

In her book *Presence*, Harvard Professor Amy Cuddy talks about the effect that posture can have on cortisol and testosterone levels and the resulting emotions and behavior. When you assume a posture that is upright, open, and expansive, you'll tend to also feel that way emotionally. On the other hand, when you assume a posture that is closed, shrinking, and submissive, you'll tend to feel and act less confidently.

Here are two simple "power poses" to try:

- Stand tall with a wide base, putting your hands on your hips like Wonder Woman or Superman.
- Stand tall with both arms in a victory pose. Hold the pose for two minutes to help you embody a feeling of confidence, especially before a challenging activity.

Confident Movement

Whether it's dancing, yoga, boxing, weight training, walking, running, or something else, physical activity of any kind can boost your confidence and self-esteem. Expressing yourself through movement, developing a physical skill, flexing your muscles, moving heavy objects, and physically getting stronger can all increase confidence.

 **UP YOUR OPTIMISM GAME: COACH'S CORNER** 

If your confidence muscles are weak, it may take time to build them up. Give yourself grace, and keep at it for five minutes a day. As you work to improve, lean into self-love rather than self-criticism—beating yourself up will only weaken your confidence.

There is a strong and confident person inside you who just needs to be developed and unleashed. Focus on your successes. Focus on your strengths. Stand tall. Have faith. Keep your head up and your shoulders back. You can do it. You got this!

NINETEEN

COURAGE MUSCLES

*"Courage is the most important of
all the virtues because without
courage, you can't practice any
other virtue consistently."*
—MAYA ANGELOU

MY CLIENT CYNTHIA SPENT YEARS IN A BROKEN, stressful, and unfulfilling marriage. In addition to being unfaithful, her husband was not kind or attentive to her needs, and much of the time, it felt like they were living separate lives while under the same roof. But Cynthia felt stuck and was afraid to leave. As a result, she lived in a perpetual state of stress and depression.

Then, she started a simple routine: First thing every morning and every night before bed, she would pray for the strength and courage to face her fear. She knew what she had to do, and after praying about it consistently, she finally decided to leave. As soon as she made the decision, a huge weight was lifted. She immediately felt energized and encouraged.

Moving on involves risks, but sometimes it's the only way to feel emotionally free. You may be in a relationship or job that is woefully unfulfilling and not aligned with your values and needs; if this is the case, you'll need to call up your courage to face the situation with strength and grace. In fact, making any kind of change or going against the grain requires using your courage muscles.

Courageously Navigating the Push and Pull of Life

You will feel your best emotionally when you're living in line with your values. But there will always be a push and pull between fitting in or standing out, going with the flow or charting your own path. Relationships, work, and society may push you in directions that don't align with your deepest values, hopes, and dreams. So, you'll need the courage to start, to keep going, to quit or change course, to speak up, to stand out, and to trust. In order to live your best life, you will need to act courageously.

Courage and confidence are related muscles because they both inspire you to take action and pursue your goals, but they each play a unique role. When you build up your confidence muscles through practice and mastery, your fears will naturally decrease. However, life can throw you new challenges that require skills you don't have time to master, and this is where courage comes in.

Courage is a strength of mind to act and carry on in spite of risk and uncertainty. When your courage muscles are strong, you tend to feel brave, bold, daring, and heroic, and courage fuels your perseverance and determination. Life is not 100 percent predictable, so in order to be successful and achieve your goals, you'll sometimes have to be courageous.

Different Types of Courage

There are different types of courage (e.g., physical, emotional, social, or moral). Most people think of physical courage, like running into a burning building to save someone. But it takes emotional courage to listen to your heart and follow its lead. It takes moral courage to stand up and speak out for what you believe in, and it takes social courage to trust others. If you look closely at your life, I'm sure you'll find many moments when you've acted courageously.

When your courage muscles are weak, you'll feel hesitant, indecisive, timid, cowardly, weak, fearful, anxious, hopeless, and depressed. This can prevent you from living in alignment with your vision and keep you stuck in a negative emotional pattern.

When you're afraid to follow your heart, pursue your dreams, trust others, or stand up for what you believe, you'll feel higher levels of depression and anxiety. Fortunately, you can develop a mindset that supports you in acting more courageously.

COURAGE MUSCLES: QUICK EMOTION GUIDE

- **Strong**: bravery, boldness, strength, heroism, confidence
- **Weak**: timidity, weakness, hopelessness, anxiety, depression

---

Think, Speak, Write Mindset Workout Ideas

Strength Training: Positive Questions to Think About

- *When have I acted courageously?*
- *When did I follow my heart?*

Cardio: Positive Affirmations

- *I act courageously.*
- *I persist in the face of challenges.*
- *The risk is worth the reward.*

Cardio: Conversation

Tell someone a story about a time when you showed physical, emotional, social, or moral courage.

Stretching: Journal Prompt

- *When have I displayed courage?*

Additional Exercises

Create a Courageous Identity

If you believe you're not brave, you'll act fearfully. On the other hand, if you create a courageous identity, your actions will follow your mindset. Recall a time when you acted courageously. Repeat this exercise until you have at least three stories of your bravery in action. Use your mastery experiences to help you see how you are actually courageous.

Practice Doing What You Fear (Challenging Experiment)

The more you do the things you fear, the stronger your tendency to act courageously. Get on stage. Go for the promotion. Audition for the part. Ask the girl out. Start the business. Write the book. As psychologist Susan Jeffers famously wrote, feel the fear...and do it anyway.

Achieve a Peak Physical State

Put yourself in a peak physical state before attempting a courageous act. Get well rested and well nourished. Assume a strong and confident posture, and get your blood flowing. While in that peak state, use some positive self-talk—and then take the step.

Learn from Role Models (Vicarious Emotions)

You can call up a strength in yourself by watching other people displaying that strength. Read stories, watch movies like *Rocky* or *The Woman King*, and observe others acting courageously.

 **UP YOUR OPTIMISM GAME: COACH'S CORNER**

Whether it's following your heart, showing determination and persistence to accomplish a goal, trusting someone else, or standing up for something you believe in, I know there are many times you've displayed courage. And I know that you can get even better at acting courageously to create a life more fully in line with your values. So, be brave and bold. You're worth it!

TWENTY

AWE AND WONDER MUSCLES

"He to whom this emotion is a stranger, who can no longer pause to wonder and stand rapt in awe, is as good as dead: his eyes are closed."
—ALBERT EINSTEIN

IN 2022, DOCTORS IN BRUSSELS, BELGIUM, TURNED to an interesting treatment to help their patients recover from pandemic-related depression, anxiety, and stress: They started prescribing museum visits. "Museotherapy" isn't a new concept, and it's long been known that art has the power to evoke awe and wonder.

Awe is an emotion that arises when you see, hear, or experience something extraordinary. And when your awe muscles are strong, you're more likely to feel inspired, moved, amazed, and enraptured. On the other hand, when your awe muscles are weak, you're more likely to feel bored, uninspired, disinterested, and depressed. Intentionally seeking awe and wonder can help you feel happier and more inspired, and you can find them in nature, art, others, or yourself.

Feeding Your Soul

In addition to decreasing symptoms of depression and anxiety, awe adds fullness and color to life that lifts your spirits and feeds your soul. Below are some moments when I experienced awe and wonder.

Nature

I remember the first time I went camping in Colorado and gazed up at the night sky. It was absolutely magical. I never knew there were that many stars. I tried to take a picture with my 35mm camera, but it couldn't do the sky justice.

Art and Architecture

Louisiana has the Superdome, but when I went to New York City for the first time, I was blown away by the skyscrapers. I spent the whole day looking up and thinking to myself, *Wow, people built these.* I am amazed by the ingenuity of the human spirit.

Others

One of my favorite TV shows is *America's Got Talent*. And yes, I cry during many of the auditions and Golden Buzzer moments. I just find it so moving to watch someone succeed after spending years honing their craft. Witnessing excellence in others fills me with awe.

Self

The first time I dunked a basketball, I was pretty amazed by myself—especially because I was only about five-foot-six at the time.

What are some moments that have filled you with awe?

Life can be magical. And when we tune into the magic, our wonder, joy, and inspiration flow.

AWE AND WONDER MUSCLES: QUICK EMOTION GUIDE

- **Strong**: amazement, curiosity, admiration, inspiration, excitement, joy
- **Weak**: "meh," dullness, boredom, numbness, apathy, depression, flatness

---

Think, Speak, Write Mindset Workout Ideas

Strength Training: Positive Questions to Think About

- *When have I been filled with awe and wonder?*
- *When did I witness someone do something extraordinary?*
- *When have I been in awe of myself?*

Cardio: Positive Affirmations

- *I look for the wonder in the world.*
- *I seek awe-inspiring experiences.*
- *I appreciate the wonder all around me.*

Cardio: Conversation

Tell someone about something you witnessed or experienced that gave you a sense of awe, wonder, or amazement.

Ask others what has amazed them.

Stretching: Journal Prompts

- *Where have I experienced awe?*
- *When have I surprised myself, in a good way?*
- Write a story about an awe-filled moment of your life.

Additional Exercises

Go Outside

Mother Nature offers a great source of wonder and awe, so immersing yourself in the natural world can easily bring about many positive emotions. Maybe it's the ocean, a mountain, or the night sky. Maybe it's a flower, tree, or bird. Simply go outside and look for what amazes you about the natural world.

Watch People Do Extraordinary Things

Whether in person or via technology, watch people who have poured their lives into developing a craft (e.g., athletes, dancers, musicians, magicians, or comedians). When possible, go to live events to be fully immersed in the experience.

You can also find awe in everyday activities: a mom skillfully juggling kids while doing errands, a janitor cheerfully and diligently keeping a space beautiful, or a young person willing to pitch in and help someone else. Look for opportunities to be amazed by others.

 **UP YOUR OPTIMISM GAME: COACH'S CORNER** 

Awe provides a spark for your soul. So, if you've been feeling dull, look for opportunities to inject some wonder into your life. You can find inspiration in nature, art, or people, and continually witnessing beauty and brilliance may inspire you to create your own magic.

Use awe to light your fire. Then, go after your dreams, share your story, and use your talents. You can be the one who inspires others. Your creativity, determination, and love can light the way for someone else, and in the process, you might even amaze yourself.

TWENTY-ONE

SERENITY AND ACCEPTANCE MUSCLES

*"God, grant me the serenity to accept
the things I cannot change, the courage
to change the things I can, and the
wisdom to know the difference."*
—SERENITY PRAYER

BEING FROM THE "BIG EASY," I HAVE A GREAT BUILT-in chill switch. When things start swirling around me, I can just flip into chill mode. Having lived in Boston for more than twenty-five years, I say this affectionately: Bostonians don't always have working chill switches. If yours isn't working at its best either, you can become cooler, calmer, and more collected by strengthening your serenity muscles.

Serenity is the absence of mental stress or anxiety. When your serenity muscles are weak, you'll feel agitated, anxious, nervous, frustrated, or angry. But when they are strong, you'll feel calm, peaceful, harmonious, and at ease. There are multiple ways to achieve serenity, so let's talk about the options via focus, acceptance, story, and behavior.

Serenity Through Focus

One day, I decided to conduct an experiment. I watched the seven o'clock news and categorized every story as positive, negative, or neutral. Of the fifteen stories that aired during the thirty-minute segment, thirteen were negative (death, destruction, war, sickness, crime, scandal, etc.). One was neutral, including both hard and uplifting elements (a young person with a terminal illness described how she found peace). Only one was purely positive (celebrating a veteran).

After that, I did my first of what became several "news detoxes." If you spend lots of time focusing on death, destruction, negativity, and everything that's wrong, it will be much harder for you to feel calm and peaceful. You can watch anything you want, but try to be mindful of how "news" affects your peace of mind.

Serenity Through Acceptance

In US culture, we generally favor striving over acceptance as a way to experience positive emotions. Striving leads to feelings of passion, interest, excitement, and determination—and achievement ignites a sense of exhilaration, pride, and satisfaction.

Striving and achieving feel good. But if you only strive and never accept, you might find yourself stuck in a perfectionistic burnout trap. Strive, strive, strive, work, work, work—it's an endless cycle that never lets you rest.

If there's no room in your mind for acceptance, then there also won't be a place for peace. You cannot regularly experience calm and tranquility if your mindset shuns acceptance. In order to feel more serenity and inner peace, you must get better at accepting…especially the things you cannot change.

Active Surrender: An Empowering Form of Acceptance

"But Charles, if I accept the way things are, I feel like I'm giving up."

I've had this conversation often, and here are some thoughts. You get to decide what is important and valuable to you. You get to decide which dreams you chase and which ones you don't. You also get to decide if you want to change course or go down a different path. This is the wisdom part of the Serenity Prayer.

Imagine you're holding a rope tied to a boulder that is hanging off a cliff. The boulder represents old stories, old relationships, and old patterns that don't help you feel good. What do you do? Holding on to the rope is painful, but letting go might also be painful, because it would mean dropping things that at one point were important and valuable to you. Faced with this choice, you get to decide: Do you hold on, or do you let go?

Don't just give up to give up. Use your wisdom and discretion, and from a place of confident empowerment, decide whether you want to let go and accept. When you intentionally and actively "surrender," you use your power to unburden yourself and create a sense of relief and peace.

Accepting Yourself

When I started working as a personal trainer, I wanted to help everyone achieve all their goals, so we would strive together! But I noticed something strange happening. I'd successfully help clients lose twenty pounds—and they would feel worse about themselves. Weird, right?

Maybe not. As Robert Holden noted, "No amount of self-improvement can make up for any lack of self-acceptance."

After striving and improving, it became harder for my clients to accept themselves. Their logic went something like this: "Yes, I lost weight, but what about five more pounds?" As they achieved goals, some clients became more obsessed, frustrated, depressed, and anxious about their bodies, and I realized that I was contributing to that dynamic. As a leader, I was so gung ho about striving to help my clients change their bodies and reach a number on the scale that I didn't leave any room for us to accept. So, we kept pushing harder, and with every missed milestone, the self-loathing, perfectionism, and anxiety increased.

There is nothing wrong with wanting to lose weight, and it can be an empowering, rewarding, and healthful experience. But after years of personal training, I realized that weight-loss goals are often about something deeper than the scale. Some of our top psychological needs are safety, belonging, self-love, and self-acceptance. Weight loss can be a misguided attempt to get those needs met. Self-love and self-acceptance originate in your mind, not on the scale. Thus, you can constantly improve and achieve but still feel unworthy if you don't love and accept yourself.

Serenity Through Rewriting
Three Anxiety-Provoking Stories

Acceptance is a cornerstone story for peace of mind, and self-acceptance fuels inner peace. Three additional stories that help you feel calm are "I am safe," "I am enough," and "It will all work out." However, the opposite stories drive anxiety.

Anxiety commonly flows from three often intertwined stories: (1) "I am not safe," (2) "I am not good enough," and (3) "It will be the worst-case scenario." The first two stories are a judgment that you don't have the resources to meet your protection or growth needs, and the third is an imagined catastrophe.

With regard to safety, your faith and hope muscles add to your overall serenity strength. Then, from an "I am enough" perspective, your self-acceptance muscles work synergistically with your self-compassion, self-appreciation, confidence, and gratitude muscles. So, exercising those muscles supports indirect growth in your serenity. In addition, your vision and dreaming muscles help you focus on desired outcomes and best-case scenarios, while your faith and hope muscles can help you feel calm by giving you a sense that it will all work out. Your stories can lead to peace and serenity, and so can your choices.

Serenity Through Behavior: Choosing Peace over War

For as long as people have existed, there has been conflict. Fighting is a strategy we use to get our protection or growth needs met. We fight to protect our family and freedom. We fight to grow our territory and influence. We want to get our way, be right, and win—so we fight in politics, sports, business, and relationships. As a result, we feel tension, anger, and anxiety.

In relationships, we threaten others because we think it will help us get what we want. But fighting weakens connection and, at its worst, creates enemies, which adds to our tension, isolation, and anxiety. Yelling at your spouse may give you temporary relief from anger, but if you make an enemy of your partner, they might retaliate. Fighting often leads to more fighting.

The good news: Fighting isn't the only response we can choose. We can empathize, forgive, and accept. Some people get frustrated with the Serenity Prayer because they don't want to accept certain things. However, the more things you view as unacceptable, the angrier and more outraged you'll be. Sometimes, you may have to fight for what you believe in. But if you believe fighting is the only way, you'll only have options that cause stress, anger, anxiety, and conflict.

You have choices that can lead to serenity. Instead of attacking, tearing down, and destroying, you can build, create, and grow. Instead of forcing others to change, you can choose acceptance and support their autonomy. Instead of demanding, you can request. You can choose ease, comfort, harmony, and acceptance. You can choose peace.

You can build serenity through mind, body, and behavior, which helps you to remain calm. And acceptance is a key to serenity, tranquility, and peace of mind.

SERENITY MUSCLES: QUICK EMOTION GUIDE

Through Acceptance

- **Strong**: calm, peace, harmony, ease
- **Weak**: agitation, frustration, anger, anxiety, unrest

Through Self-Acceptance

- **Strong**: safety, value, self-worth, sense of being enough, joyful, peace with self
- **Weak**: anxiety, depression, frustration, shame, guilt, anger, unrest

---

Think, Speak, Write Mindset Workout Ideas

Strength Training: Positive Questions to Think About

- *What do I want to work on accepting?*
- *What positive outcomes might arise if I choose to let go?*

Cardio: Positive Affirmations

Acceptance

- *I accept the things I cannot change.*
- *There is power in letting go.*
- *I honor others' freedom to choose.*
- *I choose peace.*

Self-Acceptance

- *Even though I am flawed, I respect and accept myself.*
- *Even though I am imperfect, I love and accept myself.*

Serenity

- *I am safe, secure, calm, grounded, relaxed, and peaceful.*

Cardio: Conversation

Tell someone about positive results you experienced when you decided to let go or accept something.

Stretching: Journal Prompt

What are some benefits of accepting and letting go?

Additional Exercises

"Happy Place" Meditation

Close your eyes and visualize yourself in a place that makes you feel peaceful and serene. Take deep breaths as you mentally go to your happy place.

If possible, create a serene space for breathing, meditating, or relaxing in your home.

Schedule Quiet Time

Constant stimulation makes it difficult for the mind to rest, so intentionally schedule time to be alone, preferably in nature. Put yourself in peaceful places, and your peace of mind will naturally flow.

Relaxing Body Care

Activities like massage, breathing exercises, yoga, hot baths, or spa treatments can help you feel calm and peaceful.

Intentionally Choose Peace

When there is a conflict or potential escalation, choose the peaceful route. Make requests instead of demands and observations instead of judgments. Be curious. Empathize, reflect, and seek harmony.

 **UP YOUR OPTIMISM GAME: COACH'S CORNER** 

It's okay to be anxious or angry. Those are normal human emotions. But remember, acceptance relieves tension. You don't have to constantly fight with others; you can find harmony. You don't have to worry about everything; you can find peace. By leaving some room for self-acceptance, you don't have to constantly beat yourself up.

It's a lot of pressure to attempt to change everything around you, especially when much of it is out of your control. Use your wisdom. Accept yourself and others. And practice cultivating calm through your mind, body, and behavior.

TWENTY-TWO

AGENCY AND EMPOWERMENT MUSCLES

"Agency is a divine gift to you.
You are free to choose what you
will be and what you will do."
—RUSSELL M. NELSON

A BABY ELEPHANT WAS CAPTURED AND TIED TO A tree with rope in a village. Missing his family, he struggled to break free. But after many failed attempts, he gave up trying to escape. The villagers fed him, so he grew bigger and stronger each day. Years later, a man from another village noticed the fully grown elephant and with a confused look asked, "Is that little rope all you use to secure that elephant?" It had been so long since the animal had tried to break free that he didn't know he was strong enough to snap the rope or push over the tree. So, he spent his days tethered to the tree of limiting beliefs.

Agency is the capacity of individuals to have the power and resources to fulfill their potential. Anxiety and depression are often the result of learned helplessness. When your empowerment muscles are weak and you think you have no agency, you'll feel trapped, controlled, and powerless. When you have strong agency and empowerment muscles, you're more likely to feel liberated, independent, free, and powerful.

Claiming Your Power

There are things you can control and things you can't. You can't control what people think, say, or do. And you can't control everything that happens in the world. Focusing on what you can't control saps your sense of agency and empowerment. However, you do have control over your focus, story, and behavior. When you spend energy on what you can control, you'll feel more powerful.

Another way to experience empowerment is to believe that you always have a choice. Stephen Covey popularized this concept: "Between stimulus and response there is a space. In that space is our power to choose our response. In our response lies our growth and our freedom." While you may not be able to control everything that happens to you, you always have a choice regarding how you respond. That is where your power lies.

Try Again

At some point in the past, you may have learned that you were powerless. But just like the baby elephant grew, I'm willing to bet that you have grown too, which means you have new strengths, skills, and abilities that you can use to navigate life. You don't have to stay tethered to the tree of limiting beliefs.

You have power over your thoughts, attitude, and responses, and through this agency you can create positive emotions and accomplish amazing things in your life. Even if you don't have all the skills and knowledge that you need to be successful right now, you still have options. You can learn something new, ask for help, or work to get better. And you can use your vision, self-appreciation, and confidence muscles to help drive you forward.

You have a lot of power. So, when it comes to your hopes, dreams, and passions, try again!

AGENCY AND EMPOWERMENT MUSCLES: QUICK EMOTION GUIDE

- **Strong**: freedom, liberation, power, independence, autonomy
- **Weak**: sense of being trapped, controlled, helpless, dependent, or powerless

---

Think, Speak, Write Mindset Workout Ideas

Strength Training: Positive Questions to Think About

- *What can I control in this situation?*
- *What next step would I like to take?*

Cardio: Positive Affirmations

- *I have agency over my thoughts.*
- *I have agency over my actions.*
- *I can choose my response.*

Cardio: Conversation

When in a challenging situation, talk about what you can control and the next step you can take.

Stretching: Journal Prompts

- *What can I control?*
- *What actions can I take?*
- *What choices do I have?*

Additional Exercises

Practice Setting Boundaries and Making Requests

Sometimes you might feel like you're not free to govern your own time and life. But you can reclaim your agency by setting boundaries and, when needed, requesting that others honor those boundaries. It takes vision and courage, but the reward is worth the practice!

Practice Saying "No"

Saying "no" is a way to exercise your agency, power, and freedom of choice. Having a vision of what's most important to you helps you decide what to agree to and what to decline. Say "yes" to things that are in line with your vision, values, and priorities—and a polite "no, thank you" to things that are not.

 **UP YOUR OPTIMISM GAME: COACH'S CORNER** 

I know it's not always easy to exercise your power, especially when you're worried that your response will cause disharmony. But remember that you cannot control how someone else responds. You can only control how you express your opinions and needs.

Communicate in a way that reflects your values. Be polite and genuine when you express a boundary or need, and if someone freaks out, that's on them. All you can control is making the request.

That's the thing about needs: If you don't express what's important to you, other people won't know. So, practice setting boundaries and making requests, because those actions are in your power.

TWENTY-THREE

EMPATHY MUSCLES

*"In order to have understanding, you need
forgiveness, compassion, and empathy."*
—ROONEY MARA

AS A HIGHLY EDUCATED PERSON, JOE WAS VERY opinionated about the best way to do everything, and much of his stress, anger, and frustration arose when people didn't do things the way he thought they should be done. I told Joe that he could feel calmer and less stressed if he got better at understanding others by practicing empathy.

If you're a kind and compassionate person, empathy may already be one of your superpowers! Empathy is the ability to understand the feelings of another, and it plays a major role in connection. When you're empathetic, you tend to extend compassion, kindness, and acceptance toward others. In return, you feel patient, calm, and loving. But if you feel like you cannot understand others, then you'll tend to feel more anger, frustration, and resentment toward them.

The opposite of empathy is narcissism, which I know is a strong word. The more self-focused you become, the harder it is to see things from another perspective, which leads to discord. When your self-centeredness and self-righteousness get activated, everyone around you seems stupid, lazy, and wrong. With stronger empathy muscles, it's easier to develop positive stories about people, increasing connection and positive emotions in both parties.

From Angry and Frustrated to Understanding and Peaceful

"Charles, one of the things I like about you as a coach is that you're really understanding," Joe told me. "How do you do it?"

Since Joe was a lawyer, I used this analogy: There are always at least two sides to a story, which is why a courtroom has both prosecution and defense. You can go on the attack and try to tear down someone's defenses (the opposite of empathy), or you can gather facts that support and defend the other person's point of view. Everyone is unique and has their own hopes, strengths, fears, history, and opinions. I'm a really good "defense and understanding attorney," because I'm good at looking for evidence and building a case for why someone might think or act a certain way.

For instance, one year when I was visiting my mom, I wanted to help out by doing the dishes after she cooked dinner. While she was resting in the living room, I started the water and began to wash dishes. Two seconds later, Mom was hovering over my shoulder to correct my dishwashing method. See, she's old school, and she prefers that you fill up a big bucket with hot water and soap and then wash the dishes in the sitting water. I, on the other hand, am more of a "let the water run" kinda guy.

I'll admit that my first instinct was to feel a little frustrated. I mean, I'm just trying to help out, and you won't let me unless I do it exactly your way? But then I paused and thought about her past experience (my grandmother did it that way) and her goals (wanting to save money). In that light, not letting the water run made perfect sense. So, I had a choice: *Do I prosecute and argue, or do I choose understanding?* I chose understanding, filled the bucket with water, and lived out my values of love and contribution by washing the dishes Mom's way.

Here's a key point in developing empathy: Understanding does not necessarily mean agreement. It's natural to like people who are like you. But if you're not mindful, you can develop a tendency to automatically dislike people who are different from you or ideas that are different from yours. Lack of understanding can lead to lack of respect, which can lead to hate, fear, anger, and disgust. These negative emotions weaken connection and can cause destructive and injurious behavior.

My mom and I are different people, and we disagree on many things, but I can still love her, respect her, and do my best to understand her. Similarly, stronger empathy muscles will increase your connection with loved ones, colleagues, and friends. Pausing to understand and honor someone else's opinion, even if you disagree, will lead to fewer negative emotions.

Can You Have Too Much Empathy?

Kristen thought she had too much empathy. "My greatest strength is my greatest weakness," she said. "I care so much that sometimes people take advantage of my kindness." Kristen was feeling bad for being kind and empathetic, so we worked on a reframe.

It may be useful to tell yourself that there is no such thing as too much of a strength, only not enough of another strength to balance out the first one. If kindness is one of your top strengths but you think too much kindness is bad, that can hinder you from fully embracing your value. And if you view your strengths as problems, it's harder to develop a positive identity.

This is a common pessimistic thinking trap: *The thing I'm good at makes my life suck.* It's one thing to view your weaknesses as problems, but let's not also call your *strengths* problems. Mother Teresa and Martin Luther King Jr. were kind and empathetic people who also had high levels of bravery, honesty, vision, perspective, social intelligence, and perseverance. Instead of viewing yourself as too kind, perhaps you need to call up your vision and courage to set boundaries and make requests of other people. That way, your needs are more likely to be met and you won't grow resentful. You can be fiercely empathetic and kind, lead with courage and honesty, and maintain your emotional wellness. It takes practice, but it's possible.

EMPATHY MUSCLES: QUICK EMOTION GUIDE

- **Strong**: love, connection, patience, warmth, calm, ease, sense of being disarmed
- **Weak**: hate, disconnection, anger, frustration, anxiety, depression, sense of being triggered

Think, Speak, Write Mindset Workout Ideas

Strength Training: Positive Questions to Think About

- *What are the benefits of empathy?*
- *How can I be more empathetic?*

Cardio: Positive Affirmations

- *People are different and unique.*
- *I honor and respect differences.*
- *I am empathetic and kind.*
- *I seek to understand.*

Cardio: Conversation

Tell someone about a time you received empathy. How did you feel, and how did it support you?

Stretching: Journal Prompt

- *When have I been on the giving or receiving end of empathy and warmth?*

Additional Exercises

Listening for Emotion

Grab a sheet of paper and a pen, and ask a friend or family member to tell you a two- to three-minute personal story that sparks emotion. As you're listening, write down any emotions you sense in what they're saying (e.g., sadness, frustration, surprise, or gratitude).

Then, simply tell the person which emotions you think you heard. The goal of this exercise is not to guess every emotion correctly but rather to train yourself to listen for emotion so that you can better understand how someone is feeling.

Interview Someone

Get curious, and ask open-ended questions:

- How did you become interested in ____?
- What's a challenge you've overcome?
- Who are the most important people in your life?

Don't interrogate them like you're a lawyer trying to find out their deepest, darkest secrets; just be curious and open.

 **UP YOUR OPTIMISM GAME: COACH'S CORNER** 

The beauty of empathy is that it helps everyone feel better. It has the power to make others feel heard, seen, respected, and included, while making you feel connected, patient, disarmed, and loving.

I know it's not always easy to empathize when you're frustrated or angry, but the negative emotions could be signals that empathizing is exactly what you need. Empathy is a relationship and leadership superpower, and it's one of your major connection muscles. You can use it to foster great relationships filled with love, respect, patience, and peace.

TWENTY-FOUR

AGREEABLENESS MUSCLES

"Animals are such agreeable friends.
They ask no questions; they pass no criticisms."
—GEORGE ELIOT

JOE WANTED TO GET BETTER AT CONNECTION, SO in addition to empathy, I encouraged him to work out his agreeableness muscles. The lawyer in him loved to debate, and he often picked apart everything other people said. Because he was so critical and could sometimes come off as a know-it-all, people shied away from conversation with him. Joe was not upsetting and alienating others on purpose, but he had developed the pessimistic habit of looking for disagreement and reflexively debating everything.

Highly educated people often get in the habit of reflexive debating, because college teaches us to scrutinize everything to become "critical" thinkers. Being critical and picking apart every statement is great for writing research papers, but it's not the best relationship strategy for connection and harmony. No one enjoys being in a conversation with someone who incessantly argues and disagrees with them.

This is partly why some work environments with lots of PhDs and master's degrees might feel toxic. If everyone is in the habit of wanting to be right and appear smart, the culture may reward constantly challenging others' opinions, which also means everyone is constantly defending their own positions on everything. This is a recipe for stress, discord, perfectionism, burnout, and impostor syndrome.

When you look for disagreement, you will feel agitation, anger, hatred, or frustration, and the other person may feel denied, rejected, minimized, and unaccepted. But as a leader, friend, or family member, you can ease tension and create more connection by intentionally looking for agreement. When your agreeableness muscles are stronger, you'll feel more pleasant, harmonious, and peaceful, and the other person will feel affirmed, acknowledged, and accepted.

Yes...And

"Joe, have you ever done improv?" I asked.

"No, I haven't," he said.

"Well, the first rule of improv is to always agree and say, 'Yes, and...'" I explained.

For example, as a team-building exercise, you could set a scenario like "planning a party," and then one by one, people would agree and add their comments.

First person: "We're going to throw a party with a Mardi Gras theme."

Second person: "Yes, and we're going to have live alligators in tanks."

Third person: "Yes, and we're going to have an indoor parade with beads and doubloons."

Fourth person: "Yes, and we'll have live jazz music."

You get the idea.

In improv, "yes" moves the action along, while "no" and "but" stop the forward momentum. In regular conversation, "Yes, and..." is a way to acknowledge that what the other person just said is valid and acceptable, without the denial or disagreement of "no" and "but."

"Yes, and..." can be great for brainstorming actual scenarios. In conversation, try pausing, and instead of debating, affirm and then add your thoughts. If you practice being in the spirit of agreement, you will strengthen those muscles and relate more positively to others.

Reflecting

If you find yourself reflexively debating, you can also practice reflecting. Reflecting is a key skill in coaching, and it can strengthen connection in any conversation. Essentially, it involves repeating back what the other person just said. It conveys that we're listening and trying to understand them instead of disagreeing with them.

I'll illustrate this difference with two quick examples. First, a common debate response:

- **Statement**: Michael Jordan is the best basketball player to ever live.
- **Debate**: No, he's not. Lebron James is the best.

Now, let's look at the exact same scenario, but this time with a reflection response:

- **Statement**: Michael Jordan is the best basketball player to ever live.
- **Reflection**: Sounds like you're a huge Michael Jordan fan.

Just because every statement *can* be debated doesn't mean we *should* go that route. We don't have to look for and point out our disagreement with everything others say. If you are in the habit of debating and looking for disagreement, practice pausing and reflecting back what you hear. Instead of listening with the intent to advise, debate, and correct, listen to empathize, understand, and reflect.

As you practice being more agreeable, you'll notice more harmony in your relationships and feel more enjoyment and peace.

AGREEABLENESS MUSCLES: QUICK EMOTION GUIDE

- **Strong**: pleasure, enjoyment, peace, connection, harmony
- **Weak**: anger, agitation, conflict, displeasure, disconnection, anxiety, depression

Think, Speak, Write Mindset Workout Ideas

Strength Training: Positive Questions to Think About

- *How can I find agreement in this situation?*
- *What are the positive outcomes I notice from being agreeable?*
- *Which areas do I want to be more agreeable in?*

Cardio: Positive Affirmations

- *Agreeableness strengthens connection.*
- *I look for points of agreement.*
- *I honor differences of opinion.*

Cardio: Conversation

Talk about why you'd like to be more agreeable and what benefits you hope to gain from it.

Stretching: Journal Prompts

- *When have I been pleasant and agreeable?*
- *What are the benefits of being agreeable?*

Additional Exercises

Collaborate More

If you only work in isolation, your cooperation muscles may atrophy. You can collaborate on a creative project, like planning a party or creating a work of art, or on a leadership task, like developing a project or organizing a conference. Collaboration improves agreeableness.

Join a Team or Play Team Games

Being part of a team gives you an opportunity to practice creating social harmony. You could join a sports team, a choir, or a dance team—or gather friends to try an escape room, a three-legged race, or any party game that fosters togetherness. Teamwork makes the dream work.

 **UP YOUR OPTIMISM GAME: COACH'S CORNER** 

Agreeableness is another one of your connection muscles, and it's a great way to win friends and influence people. And remember, you don't have to agree with everything someone says to be agreeable. Just be mindful of when you're reflexively or actively disagreeing and stating the opposite of what someone says.

There's a time and place for debate. But you might find that being agreeable in the boardroom, bedroom, and beyond takes your pleasure and joy to new heights and keeps others coming back for more.

TWENTY-FIVE

FORGIVENESS MUSCLES

"To err is human; to forgive, divine."
—ALEXANDER POPE

IN HIGH SCHOOL, WHEN I WAS STUDYING VOCABU-
lary, I internalized the phrase "People are fallible." Ever since,
this belief has influenced how I've responded to people as
a friend, coach, and citizen of the world. I expect people to be
flawed, so when someone makes a mistake, I'm generally not
outraged. This isn't to say I never get frustrated or upset, but I
feel those feelings far less than others because I see mistakes
as a normal part of life, just like the rain falling or the sun setting. Through that lens, it's easier for me to forgive.

Forgiveness is an Optimism Muscle because it untethers
you from past negative experiences, allowing you to move
forward in a more positive emotional direction. When your
forgiveness muscles are strong, it's easier to generate peace,
contentment, and connection after someone makes a mistake.

But if you constantly focus on what people do wrong, you'll tend to feel heavy, depressed, frustrated, or angry.

The opposite of forgiveness is holding a grudge, which stems from resentment and condemnation. It's impossible to repair a relationship without forgiveness. Weak forgiveness muscles can cause you to hold on to sadness, frustration, anger, anxiety, or depression for a longer time.

Forgiveness is a more positive way to respond to offenses, but you don't have to rush it. Take time to process negative events. When you're ready, use forgiveness to grow in a new, positive direction. You can break a negative cycle and transform relationships through forgiveness. So, forgive your parents, forgive your ex, forgive your kids, and most importantly, forgive yourself.

Forgiveness Is One of My Superpowers

When I took the VIA Character Strengths Survey, my top strength was forgiveness. At first, I thought to myself, *What kinda strength is forgiveness?* However, as I read the description, it rang true. I'm paraphrasing, but in essence it said I was patient and nonjudgmental, that I accepted people the way they were, and that I was quick to forgive when they made mistakes. Reading this, I was like, *Check, check, check.*

Being patient and forgiving is in my nature, but because I value those qualities, I've also learned to cultivate them through my mind and actions. Two core beliefs make it easier for me to forgive:

1. Patience is a virtue.
2. People are fallible.

One day, I was in Fresh City Kitchen getting a chicken Caesar salad wrap for lunch, and it looked like the lady in front of me was buying lunch for her entire office. At one point, she started scrambling through her purse so that she could rush to pay, and she looked back at me and said, "I'm so sorry."

I smiled and simply said, "Take your time."

After she paid, she looked back graciously and thanked me, as if I had just done something extraordinary. I value patience, and I feel good when I exercise it, especially when it serves to support and uplift someone else. From that place, I'm more likely to forgive—or not get offended in the first place.

Forgiveness is one of many muscles you can use to strengthen connection and feel less angry, anxious, or depressed. Accepting that people are not perfect, and working to forgive others, will allow you to experience more peace and harmony.

FORGIVENESS MUSCLES: QUICK EMOTION GUIDE

- **Strong**: lightness, relief, peace, connection
- **Weak**: heaviness, sadness, frustration, anger, disconnection, anxiety, depression

---

Think, Speak, Write Mindset Workout Ideas

Strength Training: Positive Questions to Think About

- *Who would I like to work on forgiving?*
- *What positives might I experience if I can practice forgiveness?*
- *How has forgiveness served me in the past?*

Cardio: Positive Affirmations

- *Patience is a virtue.*
- *People make mistakes.*
- *I choose to forgive.*

Cardio: Conversation

- Tell someone that you forgive them.
- Have a conversation about why forgiveness is important.

Stretching: Journal Prompt

- *How can I benefit by forgiving?*

Additional Exercises

Forgiveness Letter

Similar to the Gratitude Letter, write a letter expressing your forgiveness to someone. You don't have to send it or read it to the other person. You may simply find that the act of forgiving through writing enhances the depth of the forgiveness that you experience.

Positive Regard

Assume the best intentions in others. Most of the time, people are not purposely trying to upset or harm you. They're usually doing their best, but we all make mistakes sometimes.

 **UP YOUR OPTIMISM GAME: COACH'S CORNER** 

Feeling offended or wronged is a normal part of life. Sometimes, we believe that withholding forgiveness will punish the other person, but in actuality, holding on to resentment punishes ourselves over and over again. It may take time to forgive, but when you do, you'll feel lighter and less burdened by anger, sadness, or frustration.

Your friends and family will mess up; forgive them anyway. You'll make mistakes; forgive yourself anyway. A happy soul is connected, peaceful, and loving, so practice forgiveness to keep your heart light.

TWENTY-SIX

MEANING-MAKING AND PURPOSE MUSCLES

*"True happiness...is not attained
through self-gratification, but through
fidelity to a worthy purpose."*
—HELEN KELLER

TWO OF OUR MOST IMPORTANT PSYCHOLOGICAL needs are growth and contribution, which is why meaning and purpose are food for the soul. When you're good at finding purpose and making meaning, you're more likely to feel joyful, happy, significant, satisfied, inspired, and determined. Vision and meaning go hand in hand. Vision is what you want, and meaning is why you want it.

When your meaning-making muscles are weak, you're more likely to feel apathetic, uninspired, insignificant, worthless, depressed, or hopeless. A meaningless life is a heavy emotional burden, but your mind can find and create new meaning.

And as you get better at connecting to your values and deep "whys," you can inject meaning into everything you do.

To work out your meaning and purpose muscles, let's return to the results of the VIA Survey (see Chapter 8). Knowing your signature strengths and top values is a great way to get better at meaning-making, because you can intentionally recognize and use your signature strengths, while recrafting your stories so that you see your values in more situations.

Making Meaning at Work

If you're passionate about your job and it suits your strengths, you may already derive meaning and purpose from your work. But no matter where you are on the work-satisfaction spectrum, you can always exercise your meaning-making muscles. Let's say that your top five strengths are kindness, fairness, creativity, appreciation of beauty and excellence, and humor. You could review each workday and journal about when you displayed any of those strengths. When you see your values being used in your work, you'll feel more meaning, purpose, contribution, and satisfaction.

In addition to spotting your strengths, you can intentionally make plans to use them at work, even if they aren't essential to your job. For example, if humor is one of your top strengths, you might vow to make someone smile or laugh every day.

Lastly, you can recraft your stories about work so that you see yourself making a meaningful contribution. You could view yourself as an administrative person—or you could view yourself as an administrative person who brings humor and fun to the office to keep everyone smiling. To take it a step further, you could even view yourself as an administrative person who brings humor and keeps everyone smiling so that the office runs more efficiently and the company makes a bigger positive impact on the community.

This last statement is more meaningful than "I do payroll." There's nothing wrong with simply doing payroll or any other task. But if you work for a company, you are part of all the good that company produces. It takes a village to manufacture lifesaving drugs or create new technologies. All work can be celebrated, and if you are working, you are positively affecting someone's life.

In some cases, you might feel called to switch jobs or pursue a different, more meaningful career. No matter where you go, you can feel more meaning and purpose by spotting your strengths, intentionally using them, and recrafting stories of meaningless activity into meaningful contributions.

Making Meaning Through Relationships and Caregiving

One of the fastest ways to increase meaning is through connection. Anything you do to nurture or build relationships will increase meaning. As in work, you can develop meaning in relationships by looking for your strengths and values, intentionally using them, and recrafting stories into meaningful contributions.

Whether it's for kids or parents, caregiving can be the most challenging and the most meaningful part of your day. If kindness and love are among your top strengths, you can view each act of caregiving as an opportunity to live out those values. If humor is one of your strengths, you can intentionally inject humor and fun into your caregiving.

If you look at caregiving and supporting others as an opportunity to use your strengths, live out your values, and contribute, you can derive a lot of meaning and satisfaction from each caregiving act.

The deepest meaning will come from using your strengths to serve something greater than yourself. You can inject more meaning into your life through how you view work, relationships, contributions to the world, or service to a higher power. Everyone is different—explore paths to derive meaning in your own unique and authentic way.

MEANING-MAKING AND PURPOSE MUSCLES: QUICK EMOTION GUIDE

- **Strong**: joy, happiness, sense of contribution, satisfaction, motivation
- **Weak**: misery, depression, sadness, unimportance, insignificance, worthlessness

---

Think, Speak, Write Mindset Workout Ideas

Strength Training: Positive Questions to Think About

- *What are my most important strengths and values?*
- *What is my life's mission?*
- *How can I live out my values, even in small ways?*

Cardio: Positive Affirmations

- *I live out my values.*
- *I spot my strengths in action.*
- *I contribute to something greater than myself.*

Cardio: Conversation

- Tell someone about your values and the things that are most meaningful in your life.
- Tell someone about how you'd like to contribute and make the world a better place.

Stretching: Journal Prompts

- *How can I make the world a better place?*
- *What are the top five to ten most meaningful things in my life and why?*

Additional Exercises

Personal Mission Statement

Write a one- or two-sentence statement that reflects a purpose that is important to you. Don't overthink it. Simply write something that represents a core mission. For example, my mission is to be a bright light for others and spread a message of hope and optimism.

Value-Spotting

Intentionally look for how you are honoring your values and using your strengths at work, in relationships, and in the community.

UP YOUR OPTIMISM GAME: COACH'S CORNER 

As you use your mind to infuse your days with more meaning, you will feel your soul come alive. The beautiful thing is you don't have to use any of society's definitions; you get to choose what is meaningful to you. You have unique strengths and abilities, and you will make a unique contribution to the world, even if your circle of influence is just your family and friends. So, think about your mission in life, and use your strengths to make the world a better place.

TWENTY-SEVEN

DREAMING AND IMAGINATION MUSCLES

"People need dreams, there's as much nourishment in 'em as food."
—DOROTHY GILMAN

MY FIRST BIG DREAM WAS TO PLAY IN THE NBA, and I feel blessed that my parents supported me in chasing my dream. As a ten-year-old, I averaged one point—and six by the time I turned eleven. After that second season, the city all-star coach invited me to try out. He said he saw potential in me, and my fire was lit! I practiced religiously, went to basketball camps, and watched old NBA games on the VCR while doing push-ups and sit-ups. I practiced in the rain, dribbled in the kitchen (don't tell my mom), and mimicked shooting in bed before drifting off with my basketball as a pillow.

The next year, when I was twelve, I averaged nineteen points and was named league MVP and captain of the all-star team. I followed my coach to a great all-boys Catholic high school and sharpened my mind while still pursuing sports. My passion gripped me, and I literally had a basketball in my hands every day for over seven years straight. Basketball tournaments took me all over the country and expanded my idea of what was possible for my life.

When I stopped growing at five-foot-eight and suffered multiple injuries that made it increasingly challenging for me to be competitive on the court, my dream changed. I wanted to be a physical therapist for an NBA team and got really close to doing so. In the end, I did not make it to the NBA as a player or therapist, but that dream fueled my growth as a person, taught me valuable life lessons, and made my journey to adulthood meaningful and memorable.

Sometimes the most important role of a dream is to give you hope, inspiration, direction, and purpose. Many adults get so obsessed with outcomes and so afraid to fail that they forget life is a journey, not just a destination. Education can amplify fear of failure, because college generally trains us that there is a right answer and a wrong one—and penalizes us for mistakes.

When we have a fear of failure, we tend to play it safe and only set "practical goals" that we're confident we can reach. There's nothing wrong with practical goals, and sometimes small steps are the best way to boost confidence and momentum. But practical goals don't have the same emotional juice as big dreams. Sometimes you need the big dream to charge you up and keep pushing you forward when challenges or setbacks arise.

Have you ever noticed that when you ask a kid about their dreams, they're wild and full of imagination? Yet when you ask an adult about their dreams, they tend to be "practical" and unimaginative.

Your dreaming muscles are like your vision muscles on possibility steroids. You may be good at setting goals, but dreaming is different. When your dreaming muscles are weak, your goals can seem so unimportant that you procrastinate or forget about them altogether. With weak dreaming muscles, your ability to problem-solve decreases, and you may become uninspired and stagnant when it comes to navigating life. But you can get better at dreaming bigger and seeing possibilities for yourself.

When your dreaming muscles are strong, you'll be more energized, hopeful, and determined to pursue things that lead to positive emotions. What big dream is in your heart? There's still time for your dreams to come true, so dust them off and let them fuel you.

Seeing Possibility

When it comes to achievement, some leaders, parents, or coaches rail against dreaming in favor of "reality." But you cannot innovate without imagination. This is one of the limits of data-driven decisions. If you only do what you know, how can you learn anything else? Hyperfocus on practicality and previous knowledge can inadvertently weaken your imagination muscles. Growth comes through experimentation, so overemphasizing knowing everything first can keep you stuck. To get better at innovating, flex your ability to imagine possibilities.

Chase All Your Dreams...NOT

Because creativity is my third-highest strength on the VIA Survey (see Chapter 8), I find it easy to dream and come up with ideas. You may have a lot of dreams too. But here's the thing: No one can do everything they think about. So, when it comes to taking action, you'll have to narrow your focus to decrease overwhelm and frustration. Working out your dreaming muscles is more about strengthening your ability to imagine different possibilities than about creating every outcome.

If you feel like your life lacks a spark or you're stuck in a rut, daydreaming and imagining possibilities could be a great way to teach your brain to creatively brainstorm. When you walk through life with a sense of possibility, you'll feel more hopeful and become more skilled at spotting opportunities to grow. Plus, thinking about possibilities can be fun and energizing. So, dream for the sake of dreaming.

DREAMING AND IMAGINATION MUSCLES: QUICK EMOTION GUIDE

- **Strong**: hope, energy, creativity, inspiration
- **Weak**: hopelessness, apathy, stagnation, unimaginativeness, boredom

Think, Speak, Write Mindset Workout Ideas

Strength Training: Positive Questions to Think About

- *What would I dare to do if I knew I could not fail?*
- *What big dreams do I have for my life?*

Cardio: Positive Affirmations

- *I dream big dreams.*
- *My hopes and dreams are possible.*
- *If I can dream it, I can achieve it.*

Cardio: Conversation

Tell a trusted person about your wildest dreams. Request that they just listen and don't pressure you to do anything.

Stretching: Journal Prompts

- *What is one dream that, if I reached it, would be a crowning achievement in my life?*
- *What are five possible dreams I have for myself?*

Additional Exercises

Visualizing Your Future Self

Pick a time in the future, whether six months or ten years from now, and visualize what your life would be like if you were successful in accomplishing your dream.

Make a Bucket List

Find your sweet spot between too practical and too outrageous. Being overly practical when "dreaming" is like doing bicep curls with a pencil; it's not heavy enough to strengthen the muscles. Let your imagination run wild as you dream up a bucket list of what you actually want to do and experience in your life.

 **UP YOUR OPTIMISM GAME: COACH'S CORNER** 

If you can dream it and believe it, you can achieve it. But even if you don't achieve it, chasing it could be the best decision of your life. When dying people are interviewed, their biggest regrets are not about the things they did but things they *didn't* do.

Life is a journey, and you'll feel more positive emotions when you are on a path toward making your dreams come true. So, don't die with your music trapped inside you. Go for it!

TWENTY-EIGHT

PASSION AND INTEREST MUSCLES

"Find out what you like and what you hate about life. Start doing more of what you love, less of what you hate."
—**MIHALY CSIKSZENTMIHALYI**

IF YOU HAVE KIDS OR HAVE BEEN AROUND KIDS, YOU know they are heat-seeking missiles for what they want. "Mom, can I have this?" "Dad, can we go there?" "Please, please, please!" They are relentless in pursuing their passions.

Many of us thrived in our school years because we were constantly learning, growing, and pursuing our interests. But once we graduated, started working, and had kids, our passions gave way to "practical" considerations.

For instance, in my youth, I played basketball and baseball and was captain of my high school track and bowling teams. I studied French, was in the chess club, and competed in spelling competitions. I dabbled in piano and sang in a choir. I learned yoga and tai chi and even joined a tai chi club when I studied abroad in Australia. My joy naturally flowed.

One of the biggest passions I discovered in college was teaching. I come from a family of teachers, and after my freshman year, I worked in an AmeriCorps program where my job was to teach middle school students. The first summer I taught math and French, and it was challenging.

The next two summers, I taught science, and I felt I had found my calling. After three years of teaching, I went to my academic advisor and told her I was thinking about switching majors from physical therapy to education. She heard my concerns and said that if I finished my master's in physical therapy, I would still have a path to teach, but if I left physical therapy and wanted to switch back, it would be a much harder path. So, I stayed on my original track and finished my degree.

I am fascinated with the human body, so I loved what I learned in physical therapy school, but when I started working in a clinical setting, something just didn't feel right. I felt burned out, frustrated, and less excited to go to work. So, I made the decision to leave clinical work to pursue my interests in fitness, wellness, and education roles, and I found my spark.

I became a personal trainer and led workshops for personal trainers. I taught anatomy and physiology at a massage therapy school and a university. I taught outdoor boot camp classes, and when I became a corporate wellness coach, leading lunch-and-learns was one of the best parts of my day. Because I love teaching, it often feels like play instead of work.

Even though I didn't stay in a physical therapy clinic, I am so grateful for my physical therapy education. That knowledge and skill allowed me to thrive in positions that were more aligned with my strengths and interests.

When your passion muscles are weak from a lack of use, you can lose your zest and enthusiasm for life, and you'll tend to feel more depressed, bored, and unmotivated. Passion is one of your most important Soul Care muscles. When your passion and interest are strong, you'll feel more alive, motivated, joyful, and excited about life.

Your Passion Account

Many people take their work seriously. As a result, their bank accounts are healthy, while their spirits may be low. Your passion muscles work with your vision, dreaming, and meaning-making muscles, and if you want your spirits to be high, you have to make deposits into your passion account. Here are two ways to do so:

1. **Engage in a hobby or interest**. You don't have to quit your job and pursue a hobby full-time. Anytime you read, play music, go to a car show, or do anything that really interests you, you'll be adding currency to your passion account. But if you never engage in your passions, your spirit might go bankrupt. Whether it's once a week or once a month, try to find some time to make a deposit.

2. **Find aligned work**. I know making a career change is a big move, but sometimes it's the best way to feel alive, fulfilled, and excited about life. If changing jobs doesn't feel practical, consider a side hustle or part-time role in a field that calls to you. And if you can't find paid aligned work, maybe volunteering to do something you're passionate about will rock your emotional world (in a good way).

As we get older, we can get so focused on how to pay the bills that we adopt a mindset that following our passion is not practical. And this can lead to a low balance in our spirit's bank account. But we can combat depression and feel more joy and satisfaction when we develop a mindset that drives us to pursue our passions and engage in interests and behaviors that light us up.

We'll talk more about the pillars of Soul Care in Chapter 32, but for now, you can get started with some mindset exercises.

PASSION AND INTEREST MUSCLES: QUICK EMOTION GUIDE

- **Strong**: aliveness, fulfillment, joy, motivation, excitement about life
- **Weak**: listlessness, unfulfillment, boredom, lethargy, apathy, depression

Think, Speak, Write Mindset Workout Ideas

Strength Training: Positive Questions to Think About

- *What are my top passions and interests?*
- *What lights me up?*
- *What conditions or activities help me to flow?*

Cardio: Positive Affirmations

- *I pursue my passions.*
- *I seek what interests me.*
- *I do what lights me up.*

Cardio: Conversation

Talk about your passions and interests, and ask others to talk about theirs.

Stretching: Journal Prompts

- *What is one of my passions or interests, and what do I find engaging about it?*
- *When have I experienced flow, total absorption in a task, or being in the zone?*

Additional Exercises

Join an Affinity Group

You can pursue passions solo, but from a motivational perspective, being part of a group that shares your passion may help you to spend more time enjoying it. The group can provide structure, support, accountability, and community.

Try Something New

Every couple of months, do something for the first time. Play a new game, try a new food, or participate in a new activity. Be curious. Lean into your sense of adventure and experiment with new things to expand your interests.

 **UP YOUR OPTIMISM GAME: COACH'S CORNER** 

The beautiful thing about a passion or interest is that it doesn't have to be popular. As long as the activity lights you up and brings you joy, it counts! Even if your schedule only allows you to engage in your hobby once a week or once a month, you'll start noticing positive emotions from the anticipation, the doing, the savoring, and the memory of the times you fed your passion. So, make some deposits into your passion account and watch your spirits rise.

TWENTY-NINE

FAITH AND TRUST MUSCLES

*"Faith is taking the first step even when
you don't see the whole staircase."*
—DR. MARTIN LUTHER KING JR.

WHEN YOU SIT ON A CHAIR, DO YOU WORRY THAT it might break? No, you simply have faith that it will support you. When you get in a car, you have faith that it will get you to your destination safely. When you eat food, you have faith that it's not poisonous.

Now, imagine that you worried every time you sat on a chair, got in your car, or ate a piece of food. There would be so much anxiety in your life, but instead you have faith in those things. Regardless of our religious beliefs, we all live by faith every day.

Faith and trust are an antidote for fear and worry. If you find yourself anxious or stuck in analysis paralysis, strengthening your faith muscles can allow you to feel calmer and more grounded, emboldened, or confident. Sometimes when people are opposed to the idea of religion, they might also run away from the idea of faith. But when your faith muscles are weak, you're more likely to feel unsafe, uneasy, anxious, or depressed. Because so much of life is unknown, the ability to generate faith is necessary for peace of mind and confidence to take a step forward.

In many cases, faith develops over time. When someone or something breaks your trust, it makes sense that you'd have some anxiety about relying on that person or object. But you can learn to be more trusting, and you can regain faith, which leads to more calm and confidence.

Trusting Yourself and Trusting the Audience

Even though Kristen has a master's degree and nearly twenty years of experience in her field, she gets anxious when asked to speak in public. With a big presentation at work coming up, she wanted to talk about how to get through it. When I asked her what was causing the anxious feelings, she said she was nervous people would think she didn't know her stuff.

As the hint of impostor syndrome crept in, we spent some time talking about how she might lean into trusting herself. I asked her about her strengths, experience, and knowledge. As she reflected on her years of study, I reminded her to trust that the work she'd already put in had prepared her to do well. Also, since everyone presents in different ways, she could trust that her way would be impactful.

"Someone needs to hear the message in the exact way you'll deliver it," I reassured her. "So be your authentic self, and let your strengths shine through. Trust your instincts, and trust yourself."

Kristen started to feel more confident after we talked about her strengths, but then she said, "What if people don't *like* my presentation?"

I replied, "It could also be helpful to trust the audience. Trust that they will be respectful and attentive."

Kristen took a deep breath in and sighed with a sense of relief. "I do trust the audience to be kind, and I trust the work that I've put in over the years," she said.

If you're feeling anxious about doing something, look at yourself optimistically to build up faith in yourself. Think about your strengths, experience, hard work, and past successes as evidence of the sturdiness of your metaphorical chair. And if you're interacting with people, also place some faith in them.

Trusting Your Body, Your Doctors, and a Higher Power

At sixty-one years old, Clarence was diagnosed with prostate cancer, and his emotional world got turned upside down. He had been an athlete and was pretty healthy for his whole adult life, but now he was having a hard time sleeping and was feeling anxious. He and I had been working together for over a year, and when he told me about the diagnosis, I could hear some frustration and disappointment in his voice.

"Charles, all these years, I've been trying to eat healthy and exercise, and I still got cancer. I'm actually a little mad at my body, and I'm really nervous about what comes next," he told me. "I've got a follow-up appointment next week and surgery scheduled in a month. And I need some help calming down and getting through it."

I took Clarence through some deep breathing to help him settle, and then we talked about building up faith in his body, his doctors, and a higher power. "Being mad at your body can decrease your ability to heal, so it's important to have faith in your body," I advised. "You've had injuries in the past, and your body healed. Think to yourself, *I trust my body. I am a quick healer. My body will heal.*"

It was easier for Clarence to place faith in his doctors because he told me he had one of the top specialists. I suggested that if he felt anxious about the surgery, he could remind himself of that fact. Then, we had a conversation about his Christian faith, and I asked him what role it might play in stopping him from feeling anxious.

"Now that you ask, I think I could spend a little more time reading the Bible and praying to ease my mind," he said. Clarence took out his smartphone and searched for Bible verses about healing. After a few moments, he said, "I think this will be one of my mantras: 'Heal me, O Lord, and I shall be healed; save me, and I shall be saved: for thou art my praise.'"* Then he asked, "Do you have any thoughts about how I can turn this all into a Mindset Workout?"

"I think it's always great to use your instincts and choose what really resonates with you," I said, "but here are three quick affirmations that you can go to when you're feeling anxious about the diagnosis and surgery: *I trust my body. I trust my doctors. I trust in the Lord.*"

Clarence shook my hand and said he would work on using his faith muscles to get him through the surgery.

---

* Jeremiah 17:14 (KJV)

Faith can come in many forms: faith in yourself, faith in others, faith in objects or technology, and faith in a higher power. No matter how intelligent you are, there will always be things you don't know—and fear of the unknown can lead to anxiety and worry. But strong faith muscles, regardless of what you put your trust in, can help you feel safe, calm, confident, and at peace.

FAITH MUSCLES: QUICK EMOTION GUIDE

- **Strong**: safety, confidence, trust, peace, assurance, calm
- **Weak**: insecurity, skepticism, unsteadiness, unease, anxiety, depression

---

Think, Speak, Write Mindset Workout Ideas

Strength Training: Positive Questions to Think About

- *When have I acted on faith?*
- *When have others come through in the past?*
- *When have I come through in the past?*

Cardio: Positive Affirmations

- *I trust myself.*
- *I trust my body.*
- *I trust others.*
- *I trust the universe.*
- *I trust in the Lord (or my higher power).*

Cardio: Conversation

- Tell someone a story about a time when you acted on faith.
- Tell someone what gives you faith.

Stretching: Journal Prompt

- *What are three people or things I have faith in?*

Additional Exercises

Deepen Your Spiritual Practice

You can strengthen your faith and trust muscles with or without religious intent.

Notice Your Acts of Faith

Collect stories about times when you displayed faith, in order to build your sense of trust.

Take on a Challenge to Trust Yourself

Take a step to go after a goal, demonstrating trust in yourself.

 UP YOUR OPTIMISM GAME: COACH'S CORNER 

- **Challenges**: As you know, life will test you, and a mindset of faith can help get you through any challenge. If you're going through a job loss, breakup, or health problem, think about how you can use faith to get through it. Faith may not magically fix things overnight, but if you believe that this too shall pass, brighter days lie ahead. Keep the faith.

- **Dreams**: Dr. King's quote about taking the first step has been one of my guiding principles personally and as a coach. I've seen so many people get stuck in analysis paralysis, trying to figure out how everything will work before getting started. But this doesn't have to be your fate. The best way to learn is by doing, and the best way to know is through experience. If you have a dream, it's okay to research and plan, but at some point, you're going to have to lean into faith, trust yourself, and take the first step. It's the only way to shine your brightest. I believe in you, and I invite you to believe in yourself.

THIRTY

HOPE MUSCLES

*"Hope is being able to see that there is
light despite all of the darkness."*
—DESMOND TUTU

"TIME IS VERY PRECIOUS TO ME. I DON'T KNOW HOW much I have left." These are the words of coach Jimmy Valvano, aka "Jimmy V," as he accepted the Arthur Ashe Courage Award at the 1993 ESPYs while living with cancer.

"What I would like to be able to do is to spend whatever time I have left and to give maybe some hope to others," he continued. "We need money for research. It may not save my life; it may save my children's lives. It may save someone you love." A little bit later in the speech, Coach Valvano announced the formation of the V Foundation for Cancer Research, whose motto is "Don't give up. Don't ever give up."

Jimmy V's speech touched me because I have personally had friends and family members who were diagnosed with cancer, and I'm guessing you also know someone who's suffered from the disease. It's a diagnosis that calls on our faith, courage, and hope.

Coach Valvano had all these traits in abundance, as evidenced by his speech's closing remarks: "Cancer can take away all my physical abilities. It cannot touch my mind. It cannot touch my heart. And it cannot touch my soul. And those three things are going to carry on forever."

Less than two months after giving this speech, Jimmy V died of cancer. But in the more than thirty years since, his foundation has contributed nearly $400 million to cancer research, the results of which have impacted countless lives. Whether it's a personal health problem, the loss of a loved one, or some other challenge, Jimmy V showed us we can handle tough things with grace, poise, and determination. Hope is the answer.

Hope is a belief that the future can be better than today. It's a positive anticipation or vision of the future. Hope can affect your overall wellness in many ways: bolstering your immune system, lowering levels of depression and anxiety, and supporting better relationships. When your hope muscles are strong, you're more likely to feel optimistic, encouraged, motivated, and determined. With strong hope muscles, it's easier to get through the tough times so that you can rise to your full potential.

The opposite of hope is despair, and when your despair muscles are flexing, you're more likely to feel depressed, disheartened, unmotivated, and hopeless. When your hope muscles are weak, life can feel dark and heavy, and it can be difficult to see a brighter future. But just like you can learn to walk, talk, and drive, you can also learn to be more hopeful.

Finding Hope

When you're in a dark place, it's easy to develop a pattern of only focusing on the darkness—war, poverty, injustice, lack, loss, pain, sickness, and misfortune—but as Dr. King said, "Darkness cannot drive out darkness." Hope is the light. If you can find the right support and start turning toward that light, not only will you experience less darkness, you also just might shine so brightly that you light the way for others.

See the light, be the light, and then lead with light. If you think of hope and optimism as the same thing, then you've already learned many ways to find hope and turn toward the light, because many of the other Optimism Muscles directly lead to hope:

- **Vision** helps you look for what you want and hope for, allowing you to set goals that focus you in that direction.
- **Mindfulness** of your strengths, successes, resources, and support can give you hope, and awareness can help you navigate challenging situations.
- **Dreaming** unlocks your imagination and creativity to envision positive possible outcomes.
- **Self-appreciation** gets you thinking about how to use your strengths and abilities to make a change.
- **Agency and empowerment** focus your attention on what you can control in the situation.
- **Meaning-making** connects you with your values and what's most important to you.

- **Confidence** lets you look back on past successes and reflect on what your accomplishments say about your abilities.
- **Courage** means embracing the idea that the future is not 100 percent certain, so it will take bravery and curiosity to face the unknown.
- **Awe and inspiration** highlight the ways nature and people do amazing things, demonstrating the capabilities of life to create, shine, and thrive.
- **Appreciation of others** helps you notice the good in others and use it as evidence that people are kind, compassionate, and willing to help.
- Expressing, receiving, and requesting **love** gives you strength and hope.
- **Self-love** flows from believing you're worthy, giving yourself grace, and being your own best friend.
- **Gratitude** drives you to look for what is good in your life, down to the smallest details.
- **Joy** multiplies when you seek and celebrate the positive moments.
- Tapping into your sense of **humor** by joking, smiling, and playing makes life feel lighter.
- **Faith** in yourself, others, objects or technology, and a higher power helps maintain hope through hard times.

Drawing on all these muscles will help you live with hope. Look for the light. Look for possibilities. Look for the good in life, others, and yourself. Look for your strength and agency. Look for a helping hand. Lean on someone. Lean into faith. Lean into love. Lean into hope!

Once you tap into hope in your own life, you can also *lead* with hope. Be the light. Shine your brightest to inspire those around you. Share your vision. Dare others to dream. Look for the good in others. Have faith in their abilities, and affirm their strengths. Believe a positive outcome is possible, and be a beacon of hope.

I am sure you've overcome long odds at least once in your life. Maybe you got through a challenging life situation or accomplished something no one else thought was possible. Remember, it was your hope, among other things, that pulled you through and helped you rise. If you're going through something hard or have an ambitious goal, never give up hope!

The world needs hope, so by working out your hope muscles, you make a positive contribution.

HOPE MUSCLES: QUICK EMOTION GUIDE

- **Strong**: optimism, encouragement, confidence, joy, determination
- **Weak**: despair, pessimism, discouragement, depression, hopelessness, anxiety

---

Think, Speak, Write Mindset Workout Ideas

Strength Training: Positive Questions to Think About

- *What do I hope for?*
- *What or who can I rely on to get me through challenging times?*

Cardio: Positive Affirmations

- *I live with hope.*
- *I lead with hope.*
- *I lean on hope.*

Cardio: Conversation

- Talk about your hopes and dreams.
- Discuss internal qualities or external resources you can lean on to get through a challenging time or accomplish a goal.

Stretching: Journal Prompts

- *What are my hopes and dreams?*
- *What internal qualities or external resources can I lean on to get through tough times, rise, and shine?*

Additional Exercises

Twenty Hopes for This Year

On a sheet of paper, list twenty things that you hope happen over the next year. They can be hopes for yourself, for others, or for the world.

Make Your Own Silver Lining

Look for some light and possibility, even if it's something small.

Build and Lean Into Your Support Network

Hope thrives in community, so identify the people who can support you when you need it—and, when you have the ability, find ways to support others too.

Your Five-Minute Daily Optimism Workout

Now that you've learned about your twenty-four Optimism Muscles, I hope you're feeling hopeful that you can turn your stress, depression, and anxiety into joy, happiness, and peace. I know I've given you tons of ideas, and it's understandable if your head is spinning with options. If you're feeling overwhelmed by all the choices, you can start by following the program I'll lay out in Part 4. If you want to create your own workouts, I recommend keeping it simple. Pick one emotional goal to focus on at a time. Pick one to two main muscles to strengthen. Create a five-minute Think, Speak, Write Mindset Workout. Do that daily optimism workout for at least two weeks.

To help you decide which muscles to work out, I'm going to group muscles together by goals and share one last concept from physical movement. In physical anatomy, we use terms like *prime mover*, *synergists*, *stabilizers*, and *antagonists* to describe the role muscles play in movement patterns. Mental muscles play similar roles in emotional patterns. Some Optimism Muscles will be the main producers of a positive emotion, while others help out the main muscle or provide emotional stability. Also, since pessimism muscles act as antagonists, you may have to stretch and loosen up a tight pessimism muscle by reframing a negative story so that it's easier to move in the positive emotional direction.

Below are some Optimism Muscles you might consider strengthening to transform common negative emotional patterns. Notice that every intentional change we make in our lives starts with vision and mindfulness:

- **Transform depression** through vision, mindfulness, gratitude, savoring, awe, humor, joy, love, self-appreciation, self-compassion, confidence, passion, agency, meaning-making, and hope.

- **Transform anxiety** through vision, mindfulness, serenity, confidence, courage, self-compassion, self-appreciation, self-acceptance, gratitude, agency, hope, and faith.

- **Transform impostor syndrome** through vision, mindfulness, confidence, courage, self-appreciation, self-acceptance, self-compassion, agency, passion, and faith.

- **Transform disconnection** through vision, mindfulness, savoring, love, self-compassion, gratitude, appreciation of others, agreeableness, forgiveness, empathy, hope, and faith.

- **Transform anger and frustration** through vision, mindfulness, humor, love, self-compassion, serenity, agreeableness, forgiveness, empathy, appreciation of others, hope, and faith.

- **Transform stress** through vision, mindfulness, gratitude, self-appreciation, appreciation of others, serenity, love, self-compassion, confidence, courage, meaning-making, agency, faith, and hope.

- **Transform demotivation** through vision, mindfulness, dreaming, hope, faith, confidence, courage, meaning-making, passion, agency, self-appreciation, and self-compassion.

You don't have to exercise every muscle to achieve an emotional goal. For a given situation, one or two muscles will be the prime emotional movers, with other muscles potentially helping out. If you want more joy, love, confidence, courage, or peace, start by working out that muscle for just five minutes a day, and see how far you get!

Alrighty, now that the anatomy is all laid out, the only thing left to do is put it all together—and that's the goal of Part 4.

PART 3 SUMMARY: YOUR TWENTY-ONE ADDITIONAL OPTIMISM MUSCLES

1. **Optimism Muscle Anatomy**: Beyond the three core Optimism Muscles, your twenty-one additional muscles are vision, mindfulness, savoring, celebration (and appreciation), joy, humor (and fun), love, self-compassion, confidence, courage, awe (and wonder), serenity (and acceptance), agency (and empowerment), empathy, agreeableness, forgiveness, meaning-making (and purpose), dreaming (and imagination), passion (and interest), faith (and trust), and hope.

2. **Five-Minute Daily Optimism Workouts**: Every muscle can get stronger through thinking, speaking, and writing. Keep it simple. Choose one or two target muscles and try a positive question, affirmation, or journal prompt to build them up, just five minutes a day.

3. **Vision, Mindfulness, and Hope**: Transforming any negative emotional pattern begins with vision and mindfulness, and all the muscles work synergistically with hope, which is in many ways a synonym for optimism.

4. **Build on Your Strengths**: No one is perfect, but everyone has strengths. List the three to five Optimism Muscles that you feel are your strongest, and lean into them to help you feel more joy, happiness, and peace as you work on strengthening other muscles.

THE MAGIC

PUTTING IT ALL TOGETHER

As the on-site corporate wellness coach at Blue Cross Blue Shield, I coached hundreds of professionals one-on-one each year. While many clients had success, others struggled to make progress. One month, I decided to try something different. I facilitated a twenty-one-day wellness challenge, and over two hundred people joined.

At our first meeting, I laid out different ways people could improve their wellness. Then, I asked them to pick one thing to focus on doing every day for the next twenty-one days. They did—and something magical happened. At the end of the challenge, people who'd been struggling to make progress started telling me about all their successes and growth.

As a coach, I realized simple plans are often better at creating transformations than complex ones, and I discovered that the structure, focus, and gamification of the challenge format was a great way to help people grow.

In Part 4, I'm going to explain how the five pillars of Body Care and the three pillars of Soul Care can help you generate more positive emotions. I'm also going to lay out a simple six-week Optimism Challenge that's designed to help you feel more joy, happiness, and peace of mind.

You've got the magic in you to change, grow, and transform, and it's time to let it out.

THIRTY-ONE

THE FIVE PILLARS OF BODY CARE

*"Take care of your body. It's the
only place you have to live."*
—JIM ROHN

HAVE YOU EVER BEEN STUCK IN "SHOULDVILLE"? IN Shouldville, everyone always talks about what they should be doing:

- *I should meditate more.*
- *I should do more cardio.*
- *I should drink less coffee.*
- *I should go to bed earlier.*

Both Kristen and Joe were regular visitors to Shouldville, and all the Body Care options available to them made them feel scattered and unfocused. So, when they started their six-week Optimism Challenge, I encouraged them to pick *one* Body Care activity as their top priority to support their emotional goals. I recommend the same for you.

Because of my experience as a health professional, I can get really nerdy about the body. When I started coaching, I would sometimes overwhelm clients with all the intricacies of how the body worked. But don't worry: This chapter isn't meant to teach you everything about physiology. Instead, it has high-level ideas about how Body Care can generate feelings of joy, happiness, and peace.

The five pillars of Body Care are nutrition, movement, meditation, nature, and sleep. Each pillar supports your emotional wellness in different ways. But if you want to simplify your understanding of how your body affects your mood, you can think about (1) energy production and (2) chemical levels.

Hormones and Mood

Various hormones influence your mood. Serotonin is the happiness hormone. Dopamine is the pleasure hormone. Endorphins are the excitement hormone, and oxytocin is the love hormone. These major "feel good" hormones increase pleasant feelings like joy, happiness, love, and connection, while decreasing feelings of stress, anxiety, and depression. In addition, testosterone, thyroid hormones, and your adrenal glands (the source of cortisol and adrenaline) are important for energy production and can support feelings of zest, excitement, motivation, and confidence.

The five pillars of Body Care are lifestyle factors that you can use to influence your energy, hormones, and physical state. Let's break them down.

Pillar #1: Nutrition

Good nutrition plays a large role in mental health. In one study, people experiencing symptoms of depression were divided into two groups. Half of the participants were assigned to a social support group, and the other half were encouraged to eat a Mediterranean diet. At the end of the study, 8 percent of the people in the support group reported improvement in their symptoms. And this might surprise you, but 32 *percent* of the people who were encouraged to eat a Mediterranean diet reported improvement.* Obviously, life doesn't have to be "either/or"; support is valuable! But sometimes good nutrition can completely change how you feel emotionally.

Chemicals like hormones and neurotransmitters govern all our physical and cognitive processes. Many people only think of food as energy in the form of calories, but it's also the source of ingested "chemical nutrients" that influence your body, brain, and emotions. There's a lot that can be said about nutrition, but I just want to talk briefly about four key chemicals: sugar, caffeine, magnesium, and alcohol.

---

* Felice N. Jacka et al., "A Randomised Controlled Trial of Dietary Improvement for Adults with Major Depression (the 'SMILES' Trial)," *BMC Medicine* 15, no. 23 (2017), https://doi.org/10.1186/s12916-017-0791-y.

Sugar

Too much sugar in your diet poses one of the biggest challenges for your body and brain. The countries that consume the highest levels of sugar also have the highest levels of depression. Multiple factors contribute to the connection. For instance, unstable blood sugar has been linked to increased risk for mood disorders, high sugar consumption has been shown to cause chronic inflammation, and inflammation has been tied to depression.

Beyond depression, high sugar consumption can worsen symptoms of anxiety, because it can create physical sensations of fatigue, blurry vision, or brain fog, which can increase the sense of worry. And a sugar rush sometimes mimics the feeling of a panic attack. If you're trying to improve your emotional well-being, one of the first things to consider is how much processed sugar you're consuming.

When Kristen heard this information, she freaked out a little bit and got anxious about eating or giving her daughters anything with sugar. But I assured her that she didn't have to be perfect and eliminate all sugar from their—or her—diet.

It's okay to take a small step and see how your body and mind respond. You might decide to eliminate sugar-sweetened beverages in favor of water or tea. Or you might switch from snacks like cookies and candy to fruit. Small changes add up.

Caffeine

Caffeine is the most widely used psychoactive substance in the world. Instead of labeling caffeine as good or bad, it's more helpful to think about potential pros and cons. Caffeine is a stimulant, which means it can increase energy. Because depression is a low-energy negative emotion, sometimes people find that caffeine use helps to lift their mood. But as a stimulant, caffeine can also worsen symptoms of anxiety and interfere with sleep. Too much caffeine can induce heart palpitations, feelings of nervousness or restlessness, and—in extreme cases—panic attacks or seizures.

Joe got caught in a caffeine trap. He was so exhausted that he needed lots of caffeine to get through the day, but then it affected his sleep. When he'd wake up groggy, he'd pump himself full of more caffeine to wake up, which made him a little more agitated and perpetuated poor sleep at night. To help his body get in balance, we discussed trying to increase his energy with movement instead of caffeine.

Magnesium

Dr. Mark Hyman refers to magnesium as "the relaxation mineral." Some signs of magnesium deficiency include agitation, anxiety, muscle spasms, trouble sleeping, and an irregular heartbeat. Eating more magnesium-rich foods like legumes, avocados, leafy greens, and dark chocolate can provide your body with the necessary nutrients to help it relax.

But you have to give your body a chance to get that magnesium—another reason to be mindful of your caffeine consumption. Caffeine can decrease the intestines' ability to absorb magnesium, so too much caffeine may push you toward anxiety by overstimulating you and decreasing your nutritional reserve of a mineral that helps you to relax.

Alcohol

Comedian Ted Alexandro once said, "I feel like coffee and wine are my life coaches. Coffee is there for a pat on the ass: 'Go get 'em, we can do this!' And then wine is like, 'You'll get them tomorrow. You gave it a good shot. Keep your chin up.'"

Many people use alcohol to unwind, but too much drinking has drawbacks. While alcohol may help you relax in the short term, it's still a depressant. So, over time, it can actually *worsen* depression and anxiety while impairing cognitive ability. Further, just like caffeine, alcohol can also decrease magnesium—and, in some cases, trigger panic attacks. It's hard to live your best life when you can't think straight and feel constantly on edge.

Beyond the direct effects on mental health, long-term excessive alcohol consumption can contribute to liver damage, heart disease, pancreatitis, cancer, and other physical health problems. It's harder for an unhealthy body to generate joy and peace.

If you think you can't live without sugar, caffeine, or alcohol, don't worry—you don't have to. In moderation, they can all be part of a healthy lifestyle. But be mindful that every chemical you ingest affects your body, and your body affects your emotions.

COACHING ACTION: EAT FOR JOY

There is so much more that can be said about how nutrition affects your body and mind, and if you choose nutrition as your number one Body Care priority, you have lots of options for how to improve it. Here are just a few ideas:

- Decrease sugar consumption and highly processed foods.
- Limit or eliminate caffeine and alcohol.
- Eat a mostly plant-based, whole-foods diet.
- Prioritize organic, grass-fed, and wild-caught meats in moderation.
- Talk to a functional medicine doctor, lifestyle medicine physician, or dietitian about nutrient deficiencies and hormone imbalances.

Pillar #2: Movement

You already know exercise is one of the best ways to boost mental health. It helps with stress, anxiety, and depression. Below are just a few physiological reasons why.

- **"Feel good" hormones**: Exercise can boost serotonin, dopamine, oxytocin, and endorphins.
- **Insulin sensitivity**: Exercise can increase your cells' sensitivity to insulin, which helps with energy regulation.
- **More mitochondria**: Regular exercise increases the number of mitochondria in your cells. Mitochondria are the powerhouses of the cell, and they improve your body's ability to generate energy.

I could go on and on about the benefits of exercise, but the challenge for most people is figuring out how to get motivated to do it.

Exercise Mindset

Kristen was very knowledgeable about exercise, but she fell into a motivation trap. She would research the "best" way to exercise to reach a certain outcome (e.g., high-intensity interval training), and then she would try to get motivated to follow the advice, even if she hated it. Then, she would physically beat up her body trying to get to a specific number on the scale. As time went on, she came to dread exercise, because she associated it with pain, deprivation, and denying her own preferences.

If you're struggling with motivation, you may need to adopt a new mindset toward exercise. As I've gotten older, I've embraced the idea that movement should make me feel good. That mindset has changed my relationship with exercise. Instead of viewing it as a punishment and chore, I started viewing exercise as a gift—and this shift can help you too.

When you create a plan that is naturally motivating, you won't feel like you're forcing yourself. Pick something that is aligned with your values, engaging, enjoyable, convenient, and practical, with some level of accountability or support. That way, you'll be more likely to do it. For most people, it's easier to walk outside with a friend than to stay on a treadmill alone, staring at a wall in the basement.

All movement is good for your emotional health, so prioritize your interests. Everything counts, and it's always better to do something than nothing. You know yourself better than anyone else—use your wisdom when you create a movement plan.

SOME OF MY GO-TO MOVES

Because of my background as a physical therapist and personal trainer, it probably won't surprise you that movement is my number one Body Care activity, and my mindset is to intentionally move my body every day. Here are five of my go-to moves to get my movement in:

- **I listen to audiobooks while walking**. Love of learning is one of my top strengths, so listening to something interesting while walking helps me to get fresh air, move my body, and feed my mind.

- **I watch TV on a treadmill**. Let's face it: Cardio machines are boring, but if I'm watching *Survivor* or *Shark Tank* when I'm at the gym, the time flies by.

- **I talk to my peeps on the phone while walking**. I could just sit on the sofa and call my mom or dad, or I could go outside. If the weather is nice, I might call multiple people and just stroll around the neighborhood while catching up with friends and family.

- **I lift or stretch at home**. For convenience when I can't make it to the gym, I have some light equipment that I can use at home.

- **I move with my peeps**. Connection is a powerful motivator. When I catch up with friends, it's often by biking or walking together and then getting food. You don't have to always formally "work out"

> or exercise in isolation. Moving with your peeps is one of the best things you can do for your mental health.
>
> If you choose movement as your number one Body Care priority, focus on what interests you. Make it as engaging and enjoyable as you can, include others when possible, and remember that some is always better than none.

Pillar #3: Breathing Exercises and Meditation

Many people skip meditation because it's not as tangible as lifting weights or doing cardio—and they just don't "get it." However, it doesn't have to be complicated. Meditation is simply a way to train your brain. A mindset meditation trains your brain to think in a certain way, and a mindfulness meditation trains your brain to be aware and focused. Many mindfulness meditation techniques use breathing as the object of focus. If you get tripped up by the idea of "meditation," I suggest incorporating breathing exercises into your Body Care routine.

Meditation and breathing exercises can change both the structure and the function of your brain. They can shrink the size of your amygdala (fear center) and cool off areas of the brain associated with depression. In addition, meditation can reduce stress and anxiety, decrease blood pressure, improve sleep, help control pain, increase self-awareness, and help fight addictions.

Breathing Exercises

Your breath affects your body, and your body affects your mind. I once heard a yoga teacher explain it this way: You have coffee breathing, water breathing, and wine breathing. In other words, you can use your breath to stimulate, balance, or relax your body.

Coffee Breathing (Stimulating and Energizing)

When you breathe rapidly or forcefully, it will stimulate your body. One common breathing exercise that fits in this category is "Breath of Fire." It's basically a quick, short, forced exhalation through your nose. By forcefully exhaling ten to twenty times and repeating for one to three rounds, you can activate your sympathetic nervous system and energize your body.

Coffee breathing should be used earlier in the day. If you've had challenges with feeling sluggish in the morning and want to wean off caffeine, you might use coffee breathing and morning exercise as your sources of energy.

Water Breathing (Balancing and Grounding)

Water breathing is great to help your body regain balance and homeostasis. A balanced breath consists of inhalations and exhalations of equal length, such as three seconds in and three seconds out. When breathing exercises are written as ratios, the first number represents the inhalation length in seconds and the second number represents the exhalation length (e.g., 3:3, 4:4, 5:5, or 6:6).

Anytime you slow your breathing down to ten breaths or fewer per minute, you can support your body in feeling more balanced and grounded. Three seconds in and three seconds out is six seconds per full breath, which will give you a breath rate of ten per minute. Work your way up to 5:5 or 6:6.

Water breathing can help with focus and agitation, and it can provide a sense of grounded presence and calm. Anxiety and excitement are very similar physiologically in your body; both have high heart and breathing rates. If you're trying to combat anxiety or stress, water breathing is a great choice at any point throughout the day.

Wine Breathing (Relaxing and Sleep Inducing)

Instead of an equal inhalation and exhalation, wine breathing relaxes you with an exhalation that is twice as long as the inhalation (1:2 ratio). For wine breathing, you might use a ratio of 3:6, 4:8, or 5:10. For some of the longer exhalations, you might prefer the pursed lip technique: Inhale through your nose, but then exhale as if you're blowing out through a straw with pursed lips.

Wine breathing is great for supporting better sleep and is best used in the evening. If you do a lot of wine breathing in the middle of the day, it could make you yawn and feel sleepy. In a high-anxiety situation, a few wine breaths could be helpful, but prioritize water breathing as an antianxiety technique during the day. And just as you shouldn't drink and drive, don't do wine breathing when driving.

Incorporating five to ten minutes per day of breathing exercises can have a positive effect on your body, mind, and emotions. You can spend more time if you'd like, but even one to two minutes of deep breathing can help calm you down and center you when you need it.

Pillar #4: Nature

Your environment affects your mood and your health, so one of the cheapest and perhaps easiest things you can do to boost joy and peace is spending more time in nature.

Sunlight

With regard to combating depression, sunlight increases your levels of serotonin and dopamine, and when the sun hits your skin, it converts cholesterol into vitamin D. Vitamin D is a hormone-like nutrient that tends to stave off feelings of depression, so getting regular exposure to natural light plays a significant role in creating joy and happiness.

Sunlight can also help with anxiety and stress by stimulating the production of nitric oxide, which opens the blood vessels and lowers blood pressure. There are many more benefits of sunshine, and you don't have to bake in it to get benefits. Simply being outside, even when it's overcast, exposes your body to beneficial natural light.

Forest Bathing and Green Spaces

Research has shown that spending time under a green canopy in a forest can help to reduce stress, depression, anxiety, and anger, while also improving immune function. The fresh air of the forest has a high concentration of negative ions, which help to energize you. Moving bodies of water, such as rivers or waterfalls, also put extra energy in the air. A forest setting near a waterfall is one of the most restorative places you can put your body.

Earthing or Grounding

Have you ever used a wireless phone charger that just required you to place your phone on a flat surface to charge? Well, you are an electrochemical being. The earth's surface has an electrical charge, and when you walk barefoot or come into contact with the ground, you can absorb electrons and charge your battery.

Grounding has been shown to help reduce inflammation, stress, and pain, and it can also support sleep. Spending more time walking barefoot or sitting or lying on the ground could be a simple way to boost your physical and mental health.

Ocean

The beach is my happy place, but it wasn't always. When the pandemic first hit in the spring of 2020, I felt a lot of anxiety and started having trouble sleeping. I knew magnesium was the relaxation mineral, so I started taking baths with Epsom salts (magnesium sulfate) to help me sleep. It helped, but I remembered a doctor saying that taking a dip in the ocean provides even better stress relief, because the ocean has way more magnesium than you can add to a tub.

Around the same time, I was reading about the potential benefits of cold plunging. As I anticipated gyms still being closed during the winter, I thought that dipping in the ocean might also help me to better tolerate outdoor winter movement.

In April, the water temperature at Revere Beach near Boston is in the forties, so my first attempt at getting in the ocean didn't last long. But I kept going back two to three times a week, and eventually, my body got used to the cold temperature.

I also noticed that I felt much calmer, started sleeping like a baby, and, in the too-much-information category, was no longer constipated.

My routine was simple: I would walk barefoot on the beach for about fifteen to thirty minutes, often along the water's edge. Next, I'd dip in the ocean for ten to thirty minutes. Then, I'd sit in the sand and do breathing exercises while drying off and listening to the waves. Ah, I feel so relaxed and happy just writing about being at the beach!

The beach is many people's happy place because it offers high doses of nature. The sun boosts your "feel good" hormones and sets your circadian rhythm. The earth grounds you and recharges your battery. In addition to being full of magnesium, exposing yourself to colder water can boost dopamine. And crashing waves make the air refreshing and recharging.

You might think that the beach makes you feel good just because you're not working, but Mother Nature is also secretly working her magic on you when you're there. Add in some movement and connection with your peeps, and a trip to the beach turns you into a positive-emotion-generating machine.

If you spend most of your time indoors and struggle with depression, sluggishness, poor sleep, stress, or anxiety, nature could be your best medicine. You don't have to move out of the city or constantly schedule beach vacations. You could start by simply committing to going outside every day, even if it's just for five to ten minutes. Walk outside while you talk on the phone. Eat outside at restaurants. Or just sit outside to read, nap, or relax. To feel your best, your body and mind need connection to nature.

Pillar #5: Sleep

Sleep is the most restorative thing you can do for your body and brain. Sleep problems are associated with stress, depression, and anxiety. I saved sleep for last because the other four pillars of Body Care play an important role in supporting quality sleep.

Nutrition and Sleep

Decreasing your intake of processed sugars, caffeine, alcohol, and nicotine—and increasing your intake of whole and magnesium-rich foods—can support better sleep. Avoiding eating for the two to four hours before bed may help stave off indigestion and acid reflux, help your body regulate its blood sugar levels, and maintain more natural circadian rhythms—all of which contribute to a more restful night of sleep.

Exercise and Sleep

Research on sleep often focuses on cardio, but strength training and yoga can also be helpful. I notice that when I do cardio in the morning, I tend to sleep like a baby. Vigorous exercise later in the day may rev you up and make sleep more challenging, but pay attention to your own body and follow what works for you.

Breathing Exercises and Sleep

Meditating in the morning or early in the day can support better sleep at night, and you can also use breathing exercises to help you wind down at night. Breathwork can train your body and mind to relax.

Nature and Sleep

Getting natural light exposure first thing in the morning sets your circadian rhythm and melatonin timing. Melatonin is your major sleep hormone, and when your circadian rhythm aligns with nature, your body will start to release melatonin shortly after the sun goes down. Exposing yourself to artificial blue light (from phones and computers) later in the day can delay your melatonin release. When your eyes take in blue light, your brain says, "Oh, wait, the sun is still out—it's not time to fall asleep yet!" Based on those cues, it turns off your melatonin.

When monitoring insomniacs, researchers found that they did not start releasing melatonin until after midnight. They also found that taking insomniacs camping for a weekend and exposing them only to natural light shifted their melatonin release up to two hours earlier.*

As you work to improve your sleep, you can try any Body Care activity and see how you respond, but increasing natural light exposure and decreasing evening artificial blue light from tech devices could be helpful.

COACHING ACTION: SLEEP LIKE A BABY

If you choose sleep as your number one Body Care priority, here are some ideas to consider:

---

* E.R. Stothard et al., "Circadian Entrainment to the Natural Light-Dark Cycle Across Seasons and the Weekend," *Current Biology* 27, no. 4 (Feb. 2017): 508–13, https://doi.org/10.1016/j.cub.2016.12.041.

1. Aim to go to bed and wake up around the same time each day.
2. Set a bedtime alarm to cue yourself to wind down and head to bed.
3. Take a hot Epsom salts bath at night.
4. Avoid using a phone or computer in bed.
5. Keep your bedroom dark, cool, and quiet.
6. Sleep masks, special shades, and ambient-noise machines may help create an environment more conducive to deep sleep.
7. Not getting enough oxygen prevents deep sleep; take care of your sinuses so that you can breathe through your nose.

Your Body Care Plan:
Body Care and Positive Emotions

You may already be doing really well with a Body Care pillar like movement, nutrition, or sleep. If this is the case, you can use your current habit pattern as your anchor. No need to add more to your to-do list.

For her Body Care focus, Kristen picked exercise. To get out of her previous motivation trap, she decided to prioritize movement outside with other people, so she joined a small running group. Joe picked breathing exercises as his first priority and movement as his second. He grew to enjoy meditation and would even take breathing breaks at work.

Daily vs. Weekly Goals

Once you have your priority pillar, my recommendation is to set a daily intention around it. Weekly goals are great, but when you say you'll do something three times a week, you have more room to debate with yourself and put your goal off when Monday comes around. Then, by Saturday, you may find you've spent zero days working toward your goal (no judgment!).

With a daily goal, the question in your brain shifts from *whether* you'll do it to *how and when*. If you miss a day, it's okay—just try the next day.

Here are some sample daily intentions based on the five pillars:

1. Eat a certain number of fruits and veggies every day.
2. Get seven thousand steps a day, or do five to ten minutes of intentional movement.
3. Do breathing exercises for a minimum of five minutes every day.
4. Go outside and get natural light exposure for five to ten minutes every day.
5. Aim to be in bed by a certain time every night.

Your daily goal should be small and not overwhelming. The idea is to keep you in the habit of doing something to take care of your body. If you want, you can also use a weekly goal for bigger, more time-consuming activities.

Your mind is powerful, but remember your joy, happiness, and peace also come from your body. If you eat tons of processed foods, never move your body, load up on caffeine, rarely go outside, and barely sleep, it's going to be much harder to feel your best emotionally. So, you'll need some Body Care to unlock your positive emotions.

Want to feel more joyful? Eat less sugar, eat more whole foods, and move your body, especially in nature. Want to feel more relaxed? Consume less caffeine and alcohol, eat more whole foods, meditate, spend time in nature, and sleep like a baby.

If you want to be optimistic, your body has to be capable of generating positive emotions. But you don't have to be in perfect physical condition to feel good emotionally, so don't feel pressure to maximize every pillar. My goal in sharing the five pillars is to give you options. As you work to become healthier, lean into your number one Body Care activity, give yourself grace, and do your best.

 UP YOUR OPTIMISM GAME: COACH'S CORNER 

Having a number one priority helps your brain to focus, and this is important for behavior change. If you're trying to juggle five balls at once, there's a bigger chance you'll drop all of them.

What Body Care activity do you want to anchor your positive emotions to? It can be something you are already good at doing, so you don't have to add to your list.

In practice, you can have a second option as a plan B, but pick the thing that you want to focus on the most as your plan A.

Fill in the blank: *My number one priority Body Care activity is ________.*

THIRTY-TWO

THE THREE PILLARS OF SOUL CARE

*"Be fearless in the pursuit of what
sets your soul on fire."*
—JENNIFER LEE

ONE DAY ON A WALK, I CAME ACROSS A TREE THAT caught my eye. It wasn't very tall, probably just twelve to fifteen feet high. The base was solid, but the trunk split in two and grew in different directions, creating a V shape. One side was gnarly, branchless, and flowerless, and I thought to myself, *This tree has been through some things!* Yet the other side had lots of branches that were littered with bright purple flowers. I thought to myself, *Despite all the hardship of life, she decided to bloom anyway!*

Like the tree, you may have gone through some things that have burdened your spirit, drained your energy, or weakened your soul, but I bet there are still seeds of beauty, wonder, and life inside you. So, send down your roots, look toward the light, and bloom anyway.

If you want to feel more joy, happiness, and peace, feed your soul. Plants need water, sun, and soil to thrive, and to live your best life, you need to flow, connect, and contribute. With all the responsibilities of life, your spirit may start to wither as you're uprooted from the things you need to thrive, but with a little Soul Care, you can bounce back and bloom again.

In addition to your number one Body Care priority, I suggest that you choose one Soul Care priority to help you build more joy and peace. You don't have to do anything dramatic; I just want you to work at developing the habit of regularly feeding your soul in whichever way you feel called to do so.

For her Soul Care activity, Kristen picked singing and playing guitar. She tried to sing and play as often as she could, even if it was just five minutes to sing one song. As she leaned into her passion for music, she noticed her joy coming back.

Joe picked volunteering to serve meals at a shelter. Even though he only went once a month, it started to change the way he looked at the world. Being around other compassionate people helped Joe to develop more hope for humanity, and giving back to his community gave him a sense of joy and pride.

Your passions, interests, and values may be different from Kristen's or Joe's, so as you contemplate your number one Soul Care priority, make sure it's something that gives *you* joy and makes your heart sing.

Flow, Connection, Contribution:
The Three Pillars of Soul Care

The three pillars of Soul Care are flow, connection, and contribution. Any one of the pillars can dramatically improve your emotional wellness. Let's discuss options for integrating them into your life.

Flow (and Play)

Have you ever tried to drag a kid away from a playground while they're playing with friends or attempted to get a teenager to stop playing video games with their cousins? According to positive psychology pioneer Mihaly Csikszentmihalyi, flow is the optimal state in which we feel our happiest. From a neurochemical perspective, when you're in flow, your brain is flooded with "feel good" hormones like dopamine, serotonin, anandamide, and endorphins. That's why it's so hard to stop a kid from playing.

Flow is all about mental engagement. When you're in flow, you're so absorbed in a task that hours seem like minutes. Wrapped up in the present moment, you'll find your self-consciousness fades away and nothing external matters. In Csikszentmihalyi's model, flow is related to skill and challenge. It's best achieved when the challenge of the activity equals your skill level. If the challenge is high but your skill is low, you'll feel anxious and worried. If the challenge is low and your skill is high, you'll be bored and apathetic.

Interestingly, some studies suggest that while watching television, viewers' moods can shift slightly toward depression.

Because it doesn't take any skill to sit and watch TV, it's easy to become bored and feel blah. It's harder to generate flow when you're not actively doing something. As Csikszentmihalyi put it, "The best moments in our lives are not the passive, receptive, relaxing times...the best moments usually occur when a person's body or mind is stretched to its limits in voluntary effort to accomplish something difficult and worthwhile."

I know when you're stressed out and overwhelmed, you might just want to veg on the couch and binge Netflix—and there is a time and a place for relaxing and doing something mindless. But if you're trying to generate positive emotions like joy and happiness, it's better to choose leisure activities that help you find your flow.

Art, games, hobbies, and interests of any kind can lead to flow—dance, music, painting, running, basketball, Ping-Pong, knitting, cooking, gardening, reading, and so on. Any activity can lead to flow if it is intrinsically interesting and engaging to you.

I grew up in a family that played games like Monopoly, Spades, Nertz, Scattergories, and Boggle. I spent many nights up till 2:00 a.m. playing games with my cousins. As an adult, I still find that game nights with my peeps totally feed my soul.

As you think about flow, consider nonphysical flow activities like reading or playing cards, as well as physical flow activities like dancing or running. No matter which activities you choose, a little flow and play can feed your soul and boost your joy and happiness.

COACHING ACTION: FIND YOUR FLOW

- List your top five go-to nonphysical flow activities.
- List your top five go-to physical flow activities.

Connection

Connection is vital for physical and mental well-being. Loneliness is a risk factor for heart disease, and babies who aren't held fail to thrive. Social connection is one of the strongest protective factors against depression. If you choose this pillar as your number one Soul Care priority, you can focus on building new connections or nurturing existing relationships.

Connect with Family

You might be one of the millions of professionals who moved away for college or work. Even if you get along with your parents, between work, kids, and living life, you may find it's hard to regularly keep in touch, let alone visit them.

I fell out of the habit of staying connected to Mom and Dad, and when I got divorced in my early thirties, I felt homesick for the first time. One of the things that fueled my homesickness and depression was living alone for the first time in my life. After struggling with depression for nearly a year, I went back home for the holidays, and hugging my mom changed something in me. Just being in the same space with her gave me a boost.

We both got used to not seeing each other often, and some-times you don't know how much you need certain connections until you get a high dose and realize you were operating with your emotional battery only partly charged. You might find that focusing on being in better touch with your parents or other family members really feeds your soul.

Anchor Connection Points and Connection Rituals

In addition to your family members, you might want to nur-ture the relationship with your partner, kids, or friends. An anchor connection point is any time during the year when you commit to being with someone. Think birthdays, holidays, or other days you turn into traditions. You might set three to four anchor dates for your family and one to two for your friends. You can drop as many anchors as you want, but when you're busy, you might start with just a few times a year that you ini-tially commit to visiting your faraway peeps.

Connection rituals are ways to help you habituate your connection activities. At one time, because of our schedules, I called my mom every Wednesday on my way home from work. It became a reflex that every time I left Quincy and hit 93 North toward Boston, my brain said, *Call Mom*. Once you develop a ritual, it's easier to stay in the habit of keeping in touch.

If you live nearby, you might pick in-person rituals like Sunday dinners, game nights, or movie nights. Finding ways to flow and play with your peeps is good for your spirit. You already know how to connect, so do it in whatever way works best for you and your people.

Connection as a Mental Skill

To boost your motivation to connect, do some connection mindset work. Use your appreciation of others, empathy, forgiveness, agreeableness, love, and faith muscles to draw yourself closer to others and express optimism and positivity so that they, in turn, draw closer to you.

Other Levels of Connection

In addition to social connection, you can feed your soul by connecting to self, nature, or a higher power. You might spend some time in contemplation to connect with yourself. Or you might journal about your values, hopes, and dreams to realign your mind with your core self. Connecting with nature is good for your body, and it can be equally good for your soul. Being immersed in a forest or a natural body of water can make you feel like you're one with the earth. And if you are a spiritual or religious person, you can feed your soul by leaning into your faith and connecting more deeply with your higher power.

There are many ways to increase your feeling of connection, and this Soul Care pillar can help you feel more joy, love, and peace.

Contribution

Contributing is superfood for your soul, and you'll feel your best emotionally when you use your strengths in service of something greater than yourself.

Make the World a Better Place (One Act at a Time)

When I graduated, I wanted to be part of the reason the obesity curve turned down. Initially, I was optimistic that my contribution as a physical therapist, personal trainer, and health educator would make a huge impact. I was so motivated to make a difference that I often worked seven days a week.

However, after a few years of working in a field I loved, I started to get cynical and jaded. Some of my patients didn't get better. Some of my clients didn't lose weight, and the obesity curve kept going upward. I spent so much time looking at my clients' failures and aggregated biometric data that I started feeling like I wasn't making a difference. One of the most soul-crushing experiences is feeling like your hard work is for nothing.

Then, I heard the story of the little girl and the starfish, and it changed my perspective. If you don't know the story, it goes something like this: As a little girl is walking along the beach, she sees lots of starfish baking in the hot sun, so she decides to help them out by tossing them back into the ocean. She continues along, joyfully picking up starfish and returning them to the water.

Then, she comes across an old man who asks, "What are you doing?"

She replies, "I'm saving starfish."

"Don't you see how big this beach is?" the old man retorts. "It's miles long, and there are thousands of starfish. There's no way you can possibly make a difference."

The little girl reaches down, picks up a starfish, smiles, and says, "I can make a difference to this one," as she tosses it back into the ocean.

Sometimes, we make ourselves cynical and depressed by looking at the magnitude of the beach and downplaying our contribution, but every positive act adds value to the world. Every day that you show up to work, support a family member, lift up a friend, create art, or save a starfish, you are making the world a better place. It can be hard to see the full effect of your single act because you never know how far your positivity ripple will spread.

At times, I have been the starfish who needed someone to pick me up and throw me back in the ocean. In high school, I applied early and accepted an offer from St. Louis University before ever visiting the campus. But when I went to visit, I didn't instantly fall in love. In fact, I thought I'd made a mistake. Then, I received a letter from Boston University saying that the admissions committee thought I'd be a good candidate for the engineering school. While I didn't want to become an engineer, when I found out BU had one of the nation's top physical therapy programs, I was intrigued.

But I had a problem: It was getting late in the game. Since my dad had already taken time off to drive me all over the South to visit colleges, he didn't have the time to take me all the way to Boston. Money was also tight. I went to see my theology teacher and told him my dilemma. He said, "Charles, picking a college is an important step, and you really should visit before making such a big decision." He could see the sadness on my face, and after a pause, he said, "I'll take you to Boston. I'm from Pittsburg, so we'll drive up and say hi to my mom, and then I'll take you over to Boston from there. Just ask your mom if it's okay."

My sadness shifted to hope and optimism, and of course my mom said yes. When I met with him the next day, he had a strange look on his face. He sat me down and told me he had bad news and good news. "Charles, the bad news is that I can't take you to Boston," he said. "But the good news is that I talked to a bunch of other teachers, and we raised enough money to buy you a flight. And I called ahead and arranged for someone to pick you up, host you, and tour you around the campus."

I still get emotional every time I think about how blessed I was to be on the receiving end of such kindness. Long story short, I fell in love with Boston University and completely thrived during my college days. If you ask my teacher, he doesn't think he did anything special. He was just being a compassionate person trying to help me out. When I asked how I could repay him, he simply said, "When you're in a position to help someone else, pay it forward."

As a physical therapist, personal trainer, wellness coach, and speaker, I've positively impacted tens of thousands of lives. I look back on that one single act as a catalyst for all the good I've been able to do as a professional.

Instead of always looking at the enormity of the beach and feeling cynical and depressed, focus on the opportunities right in front of you to do good and contribute. While you might not be able to change the entire world, one single positive act can potentially change someone's personal world. So, keep contributing and making the world a better place, one act at a time!

Your Soul Care Plan

If you wanted to, you could just focus on Soul Care to transform your stress, depression, and anxiety into joy, happiness, and peace, but in the Optimism Challenge, Soul Care complements Mind Care.

To support your mind's ability to feel joy and happiness, you might decide to reconnect to a hobby that helps you find your flow. Or, if you're already engaging in a flow activity, you might intensify the good vibes with mindfulness, savoring, and celebration. You might decide to really lean into connection to nurture, repair, and strengthen your current relationships, or you might focus on contributing through volunteering, service, or caregiving.

Some activities may hit on all three Soul Care pillars at the same time. Volunteering with your kids to clean up a park, going to play music or games with elderly family or community members, or running a race with friends to raise money for a charity that is important to you are all activities that can really lift your spirits.

As mentioned earlier, some of your joy, happiness, and peace is tied to your behavior, so to up your optimism game, periodically incorporate activities that feed your soul.

 UP YOUR OPTIMISM GAME: COACH'S CORNER 

Naming a top Soul Care priority will help your mind notice and take advantage of soul-caring opportunities that arise. If you share your intention with others, they can also support you in making it happen.

If you need additional structure, you can set a daily, weekly, monthly, or quarterly Soul Care goal, depending on the activity. Just like with Body Care, you don't have to be perfect and engage in your Soul Care priority every day. A little care goes a long way.

Fill in the blank: *My number one priority Soul Care activity is* ________.

THIRTY-THREE

THE SIX-WEEK OPTIMISM CHALLENGE

*"Start where you are.
Use what you have. Do what you can."*
—ARTHUR ASHE

PERSONAL TRANSFORMATIONS MAY SEEM LIKE MAGIC to others, but they take some effort. When a caterpillar goes into the chrysalis, it's not just chilling. Instead, it's reconstructing itself from the inside out to emerge as a butterfly. No matter where you are or what's going on in your life, I know you can take your joy, happiness, and peace to new heights by upping your optimism game.

Throughout this book, I've laid out all the tools you need to create more positive emotions, and I want you to feel empowered to do your own thing. If you want additional structure, try my six-week Optimism Challenge which focuses on your three core Optimism Muscles.

If you use the Think, Speak, Write Mindset Workout Method to strengthen your gratitude muscles, you'll notice your joy flowing more easily. When you practice doing strength training, cardio, and stretching for your self-appreciation muscles, your confidence will soar, and you'll be comfortable in your own skin. As you build a mindset of appreciation for others, you'll feel so much love and connection that your heart will stay full.

Are you up for the challenge? If so, let's go!

Let the Games Begin

Here's how the challenge works. You can score points from Mind Care in the form of a daily optimism workout, a weekly optimism exercise, and one major exercise. All the exercises are laid out for you, so there's no guess work. It takes just minutes a day, so it's designed to fit into a busy schedule.

Simply aim to score a minimum of 30 points over the course of the six weeks, and at the end of the challenge, take a moment to reflect on your experience. Let's start with a snapshot of the three ways you can score points, and then we'll break down each aspect.

OPTIMISM CHALLENGE POINTS OVERVIEW

- Daily Five-Minute Optimism Workout (1 point each day / 42 points max)
- Weekly Optimism Exercise (2 points each week / 12 points max)

> • Major Exercise (6 points)
>
> **Total possible points:** 60

The Optimism Challenge Structure

The challenge is divided into three two-week phases. Each phase focuses on strengthening one of your core Optimism Muscles. Phase 1 is a two-week gratitude challenge. Phase 2 is a two-week self-appreciation challenge. And Phase 3 is a two-week appreciation of others challenge. To get stronger, you'll use a daily workout, a weekly exercise, and a major exercise.

Daily Five-Minute Optimism Workout (1 Point Each Day)

The foundation of the challenge is a daily optimism workout that takes five minutes or less. Consistency and repetition shift your thinking patterns, so do the daily workout as many days as you can. You don't have to be perfect to make progress. If you miss a day, try your best to work out the next day.

Weekly Optimism Exercise (2 Points Each Week)

Each week, you'll get a different weekly exercise. Feel free to do the weekly exercise as many times as you want, but to keep the math simple, you only score 2 points for the entire week, whether you do the exercise once or seven times.

Major Exercise (6 Points)

Pick one of these three options as your major exercise for the challenge: (1) Beautiful Day, (2) Strengths Résumé, or (3) Gratitude Letter. Complete one to score 6 points.

Making the Most out of Your Challenge

Here are some ways to make the most out of your six-week Optimism Challenge.

Choose a Challenge Partner

It's okay to do the challenge solo; however, you might find that going through the challenge with a friend or family member enhances your experience. If you choose to go solo, I recommend finding a support partner to check in with throughout your challenge.

Pick a Routine

Use a behavioral cue or time of day as an anchor for your workout routine.

Let Go of Perfection

It's helpful to go through the challenge thinking you want to do as many workouts as you can. While the maximum number of points you can score is 60, I purposely built the challenge in such a way that you can succeed and feel better if you score at least 30 points. Regularly working out your mind is the key, even if it's just two to three times a week.

Keep Going

Life happens. If you have a tough week, do your best the next week.

Body Care and Soul Care

Use your top Body Care activity and top Soul Care activity to support your mind.

Follow Your Intuition

I provide a structure, but you can use your intuition and creativity to modify your challenge as you see fit. If you want to double up on a workout after missing a day, go for it. If you like a weekly exercise and want to do it for multiple weeks, go for it. Trust yourself.

Celebrate Milestones

Use your savoring and celebration muscles throughout the challenge. Celebrate progress and use every 10 points as a milestone. If you have a support partner, you might send them a text saying, "Woohoo, I just hit 10 points!"

Have Fun!

Upping your optimism game is all about increasing positivity, so have fun with it.

COACHING ACTION: GET ONLINE SUPPORT

If you want an interactive challenge experience with videos, motivational emails, and gamification, my online coaching program is the closest thing to having me coach you one-on-one. Visit *CharlesInniss.com/game* to learn more.

The Exercises

Phase 1: Boosting Joy, Happiness, and Contentment

Phase 1 focuses on upping your gratitude game. You can think about gratitude in general, gratitude for your body, gratitude for small things, and gratitude for others. Below are your daily workout and weekly exercises for Phase 1. Tune in to what is heartfelt.

Daily Five-Minute Gratitude Workout (Weeks 1 and 2)

Breathe. Take three to five deep breaths.

Think. *What am I grateful for?* Reflect for one to two minutes.

Speak. Repeat these affirmations three to five times:

- *I look for the good around me.*
- *There are good things in my life.*
- *I am grateful for all the good in my life.*

Write. Write down one to three things that you're grateful for.

Weekly Exercises

Week 1. Have a conversation with someone about something you're grateful for.

Week 2. Do one small thing that gives you joy.

Phase 2: Building Confidence and Self-Love

Phase 2 builds your self-appreciation muscles. You can appreciate the good you're doing in general, at home, or at work. If you want more confidence and self-love as a caregiver, think about the good you do for family and friends. To boost job satisfaction, focus more on your work contribution. Look for the good in yourself in any realm. Focus on what is present and heartfelt.

Daily Five-Minute Self-Appreciation Workout (Weeks 3 and 4)

Breathe. Take three to five deep breaths.

Think. *What do I appreciate about myself?* Reflect for one to two minutes.

Speak. Repeat these affirmations three to five times:

- *Even though I have flaws, I love and appreciate myself.*
- *I embrace my unique strengths.*
- *I look for the good in myself.*
- *I send love to me.*

Write. Write down one to three things that you appreciate about yourself.

Weekly Exercises

Week 3. Talk to someone about something you appreciate about yourself.

Week 4. Do something nice for yourself—just one small act to show yourself appreciation.

Phase 3: Supercharging Connection and Love

Phase 3 will help you to feel more love and connection by strengthening your appreciation of others muscles. You can look for the good in others in general, or you can focus on specific family, friend, or work relationships. Emphasize the positivity that is heartfelt. As you try different workouts, be mindful of ones you like and the impact you notice them making.

Daily Five-Minute Appreciation of Others Workout
(Weeks 5 and 6)

Breathe. Take three to five deep breaths.

Think. *What qualities, strengths, or abilities do I appreciate in others?* Reflect for one to two minutes.

Speak. Repeat these affirmations three to five times:

- *I look for the good in others.*
- *I look for the good in my family.*
- *I look for the good in my friends.*
- *I look for the good in the world.*

Write. What strengths, successes, and good deeds have you witnessed others display? Write down one to three things that you appreciate about other people.

Weekly Exercises

Week 5. Tell someone what you appreciate about them or why you're grateful for them.

Week 6. Perform one random act of kindness for someone.

Three Major Exercise Options (Pick One)

Since these bigger exercises take more time, you only have to do one once at any point during the six-week Optimism Challenge. It's okay if you want to do multiple exercises, but I recommend just choosing one.

Beautiful Day

Intentionally set aside two to eight hours to do something joyful. It could be as simple as going out to dinner and a movie, taking a trip to the beach, or visiting friends and family.

Strengths Résumé

Write one detailed journal entry about a peak moment from

your life, when you used a strength to accomplish something you're proud of. To score 6 points, you only have to write one story about any strength. If you like this exercise, feel free to add additional stories to your Strengths Résumé.

Gratitude Letter

This is a powerful exercise. Write and present a Gratitude Letter to someone you really want to thank. You can read it out loud to them if you choose.

Note: If it takes you a little longer to write and share your Gratitude Letter, don't feel pressure to cram it into the six weeks. If you have plans to visit a loved one in the upcoming weeks after your challenge finishes, that's okay.

A Final Reflection

When you've finished your challenge, add up all your points and look at the number with an appreciative and celebratory eye. Write a journal entry celebrating your growth and accomplishments. Below are some sample questions to help inspire you. You don't have to answer all of them, and you can add others. Just write from your heart.

- What was your best experience during the challenge?
- How did you grow, even if only a little bit?
- What positives did you notice as a result of working out your Optimism Muscles?
- What are your biggest takeaways?

COACHING ACTION: GET YOUR SCORECARD

For a free downloadable, printable version for you and your challenge partners, visit: *CharlesInniss.com/scorecard*.

SIX-WEEK OPTIMISM CHALLENGE SCORECARD

Start Date: ___________________________________

Daily Workouts (1 pt per day)

Week 1: ☐ ☐ ☐ ☐ ☐ ☐ ☐
Week 2: ☐ ☐ ☐ ☐ ☐ ☐ ☐
Week 3: ☐ ☐ ☐ ☐ ☐ ☐ ☐
Week 4: ☐ ☐ ☐ ☐ ☐ ☐ ☐
Week 5: ☐ ☐ ☐ ☐ ☐ ☐ ☐
Week 6: ☐ ☐ ☐ ☐ ☐ ☐ ☐

Weekly Exercise (2 pts per week)

Week 1:☐ 2:☐ 3:☐ 4:☐ 5:☐ 6:☐

Major Exercise (6 pts)

Beautiful Day, *Strengths Résumé*, or *Gratitude Letter* ☐

Total Points ___________

Focusing on Mind Care and including a little Body and Soul Care can go a long way toward boosting your joy, happiness, and peace of mind. Everyone grows in different ways from this challenge, as Joe and Kristen found out.

Joe's Story: Body Care, Forgiveness, and Appreciation of Others

De-stressing (Phase 1)

Because Joes's goals included stress reduction and sleep improvement, he focused on breathing exercises for Body Care and tried to meditate every day during his challenge, but he got off to a rocky start with journaling. He felt he was just writing the same things over and over. To make matters worse, during the first week, he got into an argument with his fifteen-year-old son, Chris. After Chris lost a baseball game, Joe was lecturing him about how hard work leads to winning, when Chris blurted out, "There's more to life than money and winning, Dad!"

Later, Joe did some self-reflection and knew there was truth in his son's words. That night, he went deeper with his gratitude practice and wrote about more than material things like his car, house, and boat. Looking for gratitude in small moments and focusing on breathing exercises helped Joe to start de-stressing.

Self-Forgiveness (Phase 2)

Much of Joe's positive identity came from his career accomplishments, but a huge source of his shame came from the idea that he'd "failed" at marriage and was not the perfect father. He wanted to improve his relationship with his son but worried that emotional baggage might get in the way. So, we talked about forgiveness.

I told him, "Trust that Chris will forgive you, and remember to also forgive yourself. Nobody is perfect, so inevitably we choose to love people despite their flaws. And when we forgive first, it allows us to appreciate the good." To increase his self-appreciation, Joe practiced self-forgiveness. And as he got better at forgiving himself, he also got a little better at forgiving and appreciating others.

The Father (Phase 3)

When Phase 3 started, Joe journaled on what he appreciated and loved about Chris, and he used the five love languages to show Chris love. As a result, Chris started opening up more. During one drive home, Chris started complaining about something his mom did. Joe listened patiently and then said, "You know, your mom loves you and is doing her best, but sometimes she might make mistakes. It's okay to be upset, but always try to forgive her. It's your choice, but when you get inside, maybe give Mom a hug."

"Will do, Dad," Chris said, fist bumping Joe before he closed the car door.

The conversation about forgiveness stuck with Joe all evening, and when he sat down to journal that night, he realized he hadn't forgiven his own mom. Joe blamed her for his family's problems and financial struggles, and he realized he was so critical that he missed much of her blessing. He felt deep remorse, because his mom had died five years earlier, and he never thanked her properly. He wrote a Gratitude Letter to his mom and felt something heal inside himself.

Appreciate and forgive others so that you feel less stress and more love and connection.

The New Joe

Body Care, forgiveness, and appreciation of others fueled Joe's transformation. He started sleeping better. His stress decreased, as did his blood pressure. But the biggest gift was how his relationships started shifting, especially with his son.

During the last baseball game of the season, Chris had a chance to win the game for his team, but he struck out. After shaking hands with the winners and commiserating with his teammates, Chris climbed into the stands expecting Joe to blame him for the loss. Instead, Joe said, "I'm proud of how you kept fighting until the end."

"Thanks, Dad," Chris replied, "but we still lost."

"You know, a wise person once told me there's more to life than winning," Joe told him. "I know at times I've been hard on you and pushed you to be great at everything, but achieving things is not why I love you. I love you unconditionally because you're my son."

Chris gave his dad a hug as a tear rolled down Joe's face.

No matter how old you are, you can learn and evolve. When you decide to up your optimism game, you will grow in surprising ways. Elements of your physical and mental health can change, but more importantly, as your mindset shifts, you'll notice a difference in how you show up and experience the most meaningful things in your life.

Kristen's Story: Soul Care, Self-Love, and Kindness

House of Joy (Phase 1)

Kristen was eager to boost her joy and decided to include her husband, Rob, and her daughters, Sara and Jessie, in her gratitude workouts. At dinner, they started going around the table to say one thing they were grateful for. Her daughters got really into it and often couldn't wait until dinner to share their good news.

Practicing gratitude for her body was a challenge for Kristen, but she kept working at it because she didn't want to be so negative and self-conscious, especially in front of her daughters. She could feel the entire family's gratitude muscles getting stronger, and their home became filled with joy.

Life is a team sport, so you don't have to play alone. When you involve others in your journey, the ripple of joy can impact those around you.

Igniting the Spark (Phase 2)

Kristen's family enjoyed their shared gratitude practice, so they continued going around the table during dinner. But deep down, Kristen was tired of feeling guilty as a mom. Instead of focusing on all the things she wasn't able to do for her daughters, she appreciated and celebrated all the things she was doing. The more she thought about all she was contributing, the more she started feeling like she was enough.

She really committed to her Strengths Résumé. Consistently journaling about her strengths and contributions emboldened her, and she decided to sign up for a talent show. She wanted to show her daughters they could boldly pursue their passions. By focusing on Soul Care through music and self-appreciation, Kristen's spark started to come back.

If you keep feeding your soul and practice looking for the good in yourself, your spark will come back too.

Shining Her Light (Phase 3)

Because kindness was one of her top strengths, Kristen was excited to see that committing a random act of kindness was one of the weekly exercises, and she leaned into this strength. She did random things for neighbors, friends, and even coworkers. She noticed that spreading kindness at work energized her.

Kristen journaled on what she appreciated about her mom and husband, but she didn't keep the appreciation to herself. She started texting them just to say nice things. She felt so much love, and spreading kindness around made her feel like she was making a difference.

More love and connection can start with you. One kind act can get the ball rolling. So, serve, love, and show appreciation in ways that feel true to your heart.

The Star

Soul Care, self-love, and kindness fueled Kristen's transformation, and she started seeing herself in a new light. The day of the community talent show, she practiced one last time and did some mindset work. She visualized the crowd responding well and repeated encouraging affirmations.

That evening, the auditorium was packed, and after hearing some of the early performances, she started to doubt herself, thinking, *What are you doing? This is silly!* Then, she reframed: *Singing is your passion. You are meant to shine.* As it got closer to her turn, her heart started racing, her palms got sweaty, and then she knew...she was ready to rock!

It was her turn, her time. She took a breath, and with her shoulders back and head held high, she confidently walked on stage. "This is an original song inspired by my daughters," she said. "It's called 'Gratitude.' I hope you like it."

She strummed the guitar and started to sing. For five minutes, time stood still. She was completely present and lost in the moment at the same time. When she finished, her daughters were the first to cheer, and a ripple echoed through the crowd. Humbled and proud, Kristen graciously took a bow and walked off stage.

Afterward, her daughters ran up to her, saying, "Mommy, you were amazing!"

Her husband commented, "You looked like a star!"

It was a peak moment, one she'll never forget.

That night, she put the girls to bed and kissed each of them on the forehead. While she was brushing her teeth, she made eye contact with herself in the mirror, and a slight smile crossed her face. No, she's not a famous singer, but she's respected at work, loved by her friends and family, and, most importantly, *happy.*

Once in bed, she reached for her journal and wrote, "I am grateful for my daughters. They bring me so much joy. I'm thankful that I still get to spend time with my mom and appreciate all she's done for me. I'm grateful for my husband's love and support. Lastly, I appreciate my role in creating good in my life. I am creative, brave, and kind. I send love to me."

As her head hit the pillow, she realized that she was becoming the woman she'd envisioned when she was younger. With a heart full of joy, happiness, and gratitude, she closed her eyes and drifted off into a deep and peaceful sleep.

PART 4 SUMMARY: PUTTING IT ALL TOGETHER

1. **The Five Pillars of Body Care**: Body Care includes nutrition, movement, breathing and meditation, nature, and sleep. Pick any one of these to work on daily or weekly, and you'll find your body is more capable of supporting optimism.

2. **The Three Pillars of Soul Care**: Soul Care rests on the behaviors of flow, connection, and contribution. To care for your soul, get in the zone, connect with your peeps, and find ways to make the world a better place.

3. **Take the Six-Week Optimism Challenge**: Ready to make a positive change in your life? Earn up to 60 points doing Think, Speak, Write Mindset Workouts and other exercises over the course of six weeks, with a two-week phase devoted to each of the core Optimism Muscles: gratitude, appreciation of self, and appreciation of others.

4. **Shine Brightly**: You are meant to shine! And even if tough times have dulled your brilliance, you can find your spark and harness the power of optimism to shine your brightest. You can be a beacon of love, joy, and hope—if you dare to dream and persist in your pursuit of seeing the good in others, life, and yourself.

CONCLUSION

Before I go, I'd like to ask you a few questions.

Beyond experiencing more positive emotions, how else do you hope upping your optimism game will positively impact your life?

Do you want to be a bright light and inspiration for family and friends?

Do you want to shine at work and crush your personal goals?

Do you want to make a bigger positive impact on your community?

If Kristen and Joe can change, then so can you! Whatever your hopes and dreams, remember that your mind is powerful. You can learn, you can grow, and you can shine!

I can't promise that life will be perfect, but even when external circumstances are challenging, you still have the ability to generate positive emotions. If you use the principles in this book, I'm confident you can train your brain to create many more moments of joy, happiness, and peace.

In the anatomy of emotion, you learned that emotions are created by the interplay between your mind, body, and behavior, so your emotional self-care umbrella can include Mind

Care, Body Care, and Behavior/Soul Care. Anything you do to care for your body or feed your soul will help you feel more positive emotions, but remember: Thinking affects everything.

In the anatomy of thinking, we defined mindset as a product of your focus and story. Your focus and story affect how you feel and what you do. So, you can feel more joy, happiness, and peace by shifting your focus to positives and telling yourself more positive stories.

Also, since some of your happiness is tied to your behavior, you can use the anatomy of motivation to take positive action. Focusing on positive aspects of change, like your hopes and dreams, increases your drive. Focusing on positive aspects of yourself, like your strengths and past successes, boosts your confidence. Fear won't win. You got this!

To help you conceptualize mental health, I've classified thinking patterns as mental muscles. Optimism Muscles generate positive emotions, while pessimism muscles generate negative ones. Both sets of muscles are part of the human experience, but when your Optimism Muscles are stronger and you have a better positivity ratio, you'll feel like you're thriving emotionally.

You can increase your positivity by strengthening your three core Optimism Muscles: gratitude, self-appreciation, and appreciation of others. And as you get better at looking for the good in life, others, and yourself, you'll start to transform stress, depression, and anxiety into peace and joy.

To further transform stress, consider the anatomy of stress. Your experience of stress is influenced by your situation, behavior, body, and mind, but remember that your circumstances only account for 10 percent of your happiness. Sometimes, changing your situation or doing more Body Care is the best place to start, but your mindset is often the best stress-management tool. As you change your mindset, you can go from being overwhelmed, anxious, and burned out to energized and focused or calm and at peace. And now, you've got tools to make that shift.

You can breathe, think, speak, write, and act to work out your mindset and transform your emotions. Breathe to warm up your brain. Think about the answer to a positive question. Speak positive phrases out loud. Write positive thoughts on paper. Then, act in ways that reinforce positive emotions. A little mental strength training, cardio, and stretching goes a long way.

Beyond the core Optimism Muscles, there are many other ways to up your optimism game. Here's a sample of how you can use your twenty-one additional Optimism Muscles to generate a wide variety of positive emotions:

- Focus on what you want to be, have, and do.
- Be mindful to better navigate your emotional world.
- Savor and celebrate the good in life.
- Intentionally seek joy and fun.
- Love others and yourself.
- Accept what you can't control, and use your agency, confidence, and courage to change what you can.
- Build connection through empathy, agreeableness, and forgiveness.
- Feed your soul with awe, meaning, and passion.

- Chase your dreams.
- Keep the faith, and never give up hope.

If you want good mental health, you have to work out your mind. The good news is just five minutes a day can transform your life.

Joe was able to combat his anger and stress so that he could become a more effective leader. In addition to feeling better physically, he strengthened the connection in his most important relationship—the one with his son. Despite being a busy working mom, Kristen stepped into her confidence, found her spark, and reclaimed her joy. And her personal growth had a hugely positive impact on her family.

Now, it's your turn. More joy, happiness, and peace are right there for you to claim, and all you have to do is *up your optimism game!*

Your optimism coach,
Charles

ACKNOWLEDGMENTS

To my number one cheerleader: Mom, without your love, support, and encouragement, this book would not have been possible. Thank you for always having my back!

To my dad: Thank you for all the ways you've supported me. Our philosophical musings helped me become a deep thinker, and that's reflected in my writing.

To my sister: Your creativity, grit, and faith inspire me, and your love and support mean the world to me.

To all my clients: You are the reason this book exists. Your stories, questions, and triumphs have inspired me. I've grown because of you and hope you notice your influence throughout the book. Thank you for making me the coach I am today.

To all my friends and family who listened to me blab about my book for four years: I appreciate your ears and support. Simply by listening, you helped me find clarity and sustain my motivation to finish. I did all the writing, but you totally helped. Thanks.

To my coaching mentors, Erika Jackson and Margaret Moore of Wellcoaches: My journey to coaching mastery began with you, and your leadership and guidance have propelled me onward and upward. Thank you for lighting the way.

To all the positive psychology pioneers and researchers whose work informed my ideas: Thank you for building a foundation for me to stand on. It's an honor to continue the impactful project you began.

To all the additional support personnel (editors, publishing manager, designers, etc.): I see you. It takes a village to publish a book, and I appreciate each of your contributions.

Lastly, to my book coach and editor, Chas Hoppe: Thank you for helping me bring my vision into reality. I am forever grateful for your guidance and support!

ABOUT THE AUTHOR

Charles Inniss earned his Professional Certified Coach credential from the International Coaching Federation and his doctorate in physical therapy at Boston University. In twelve-plus years as a corporate wellness coach, he's coached over one thousand professionals one-on-one and has touched thousands more through workshops and keynote speeches.

In addition to speaking at companies like UniFirst, Vertex, and NACU, Charles teaches coaching psychology for the Wellcoaches Corporation and has been invited to speak at conferences sponsored by organizations such as the American Academy of Family Physicians and the American College of Lifestyle Medicine.

Someone once said, "If a motivational speaker and a college professor had a baby, it would be Charles!" Blending a deep educational background with years of coaching and teaching experience, Charles masterfully weaves science and storytelling together, leaving audiences feeling educated, entertained, and inspired.

He often refers to himself as an optimism coach, because he believes that our ability to cultivate optimism and positivity is the most important skill connected to well-being. Hope is one of his superpowers, and he's on a mission to make the world a healthier and happier place by spreading a message of hope and optimism as far and wide as he can.

To learn more about Charles's coaching programs or to book him as a speaker, get in touch at *CharlesInniss.com* or *LinkedIn.com/in/charles-inniss*.